ANGER MANAGEMENT SKILLS FOR WOMEN

IDA GREENE, Ph.D.

ANGER MANAGEMENT SKILLS FOR WOMEN

Ida Greene, Ph.D.

ATTENTION COLLEGES AND UNIVERSITIES, CORPORATIONS, AND PROFESSIONAL ORGANIZATIONS: Quantity discounts are available on bulk purchases of this book for educational training purposes, fund raising, or gift giving. For information contact: **P. S. I. Publishers, 2910 Baily Ave. San Diego, CA 92105 (619) 262-9951.**

The author

Ida Greene, Ph.D., RN, Marriage, Family, Child Counselor has established a non-profit organization called, Our Place Center of Self-Esteem, which assists children, and families to cope with issues of abuse and violence. $2.00 from the sale of each book is donated to Our Place Center of Self-Esteem. Dr. Ida Greene is a keynote speaker, conducts seminars, and workshops on personal/professional growth topics, (619) 262-9951.

Other books by the author are:
Light the Fire Within You
Soft Power Negotiation Skills™
How to Be A Success In Business
How To Improve Self-Esteem In The African American Child
How To Improve Self-Esteem In Any Child
Are You Ready for Success?
Say Goodbye to Your Smallness, Hello to Your Greatness
Soup for the African American Soul
Self-Esteem, The Essence of You
Anger Management Skills for Men/Children.

Audio Cassette tapes series:
Money, How to Get, How to Keep It
Light The Fire Within You.

Video-Cassette:
Self-Esteem, The Essence of You.

ACKNOWLEDGMENTS

I Wish To Thank God for helping me to stretch beyond my limitations to reach for higher goals, and implanting within me a spirit of power, courage and a sound mind.

Ida Greene, Ph.D.

Contents

Foreword

ANGER MANAGEMENT SKILLS FOR WOMEN

I believe there is a natural impulse within all creation to evolve, expand and refine itself; we either stagnate and die or better ourselves and live more productive and fuller lives. All of nature tells us to change and evolve; notice the blossom on a tree as it changs to fruit, and the seasons of the year as they go from cool to warm and wet to dry. Nothing ever remains the same, including our body, which changes as we grow older regardless of the kinds of food we eat.

There is a peculiar characteristic about us humans that makes us want to better our condition and improve our lifestyle. God has implanted within us a striving to be more, a striving for completion and wholeness; the foundation on which is self-esteem, self-confidence, and faith in a power greater than ourselves. Many of us seek to make changes in our outer lives but fail to listen to our inner prompting. Yet there are others, who only want to eat, sleep, and live a life of quiet desperation, futility, hopelessness, and helplessness. We were born to procreate and create, to improve our life and the lives of others through the accomplishment of moving through the turmoil, trials, tribulation and aspirations in our life.

Chapter 1

The Female and Her Relationship to Anger

Women tend to be takers or absorbers of their feelings and emotions. They are taught as children to be nice, polite and kind. Girls are reared to be people pleasers, because the focus of their rearing is to be nice and avoid hurting others feelings. We tell girls to hold their feelings inside, and we tell little boys how they should express their feelings of upset. The problem is that we do not train boys when and how it is appropriate to express their feelings of frustration and anger. There is a point where a woman has to decide which side of the fence she is going to be on. Is she going to be on the side of the victim, the one who is controlled and abused? If she has been the victim of abuse and has decided to no longer tolerate being abused, is she going to be on the side of the perpetrator and abuser? Sometimes, a woman who has been abused by a man and is no longer living with him, feels out of balance without chaos in her life. To fill this void, she might seek out a passive man, a man she can abuse, so she can take on the role of the controller and violent partner.

Boys often decide they do not want to be involved with controlling women, because they can feel less masculine around women who are controllers. Girls and women often allow themselves to be controlled because they yield to the expression of their feelings. They ignore minor irritations and frustrations, allowing bad feelings and tension to build up causing them to erupt or blow up like a volcano. It is better to address issues in the present, while they are fresh in your mind, rather than later, when your feelings and emotions are volatile and your recall of the incident is blurred.

ANGER — THE DEMON INSIDE US

First of all, it seems clear that we have two basic ways of dealing with our own anger; we can (a) prevent it, i.e. keep anger from welling up inside of us, or (b) control it, i.e. modify our aggressive urges after anger erupts inside. The preventative approach sounds

1

ideal — avoiding frustrating situations. Be assertive when things first annoy you and eliminate irrational ideas that arouse anger. However, we can't avoid all frustrations and all thoughts that arouse anger.

Secondly, in situations where we haven't learned to prevent an angry reaction, we seem to fall into two easily recognized categories: (a) repressors–suppressors or (b) "exploders" or hotheaded expressers. Do you recognize yourself and others you are close to? The repressors–suppressors haven't prevented the anger, they have just hidden or suppressed it. The repressors–suppressors may eventually erupt in fits of rage, much like the "exploders." However, in "exploders," angry feelings and aggressive responses are immediate and there is little time for prevention or time to think about avoiding anger. The emotions just spew out. Exploders might use the same methods including learning tolerance, challenging irrational ideas, and strengthening their philosophy of love.

To help children manage their anger better, the focus should be on child-rearing practices and a humanistic education designed to build self-esteem, model non-aggressive behavioral responses and reward constructive non-violent behavior. Of course, there are times when anger is appropriate and effective. Carol Tavris, in her book *Anger: The Misunderstood Emotion*, says anger is effective only under these conditions:

1. The anger is directed at the offending person (telling your friends may increase your anger).
2. The expression of anger satisfies your need to influence the situation and/or correct an injustice.

Sometimes the best thing to do about anger is nothing, including thinking about the incident. The irritating event is frequently unimportant, and its memory will soon fade if you stay quiet. Preventing yourself from acting will help your relationships to remain neutral and respectful. When it comes to anger, you are sometimes damned if you express your anger and damned if you don't. Swallowing anger may be unwise to do on a continual basis. Some theorists say that self-instructions to suppress anger for a long period of time may be risky because it lowers our self-esteem, increases our sense of powerlessness, and increases our health risks. Other theorists point to a phenomenon called "laughter in church," i.e. holding back the expression of an emotion, likes a laugh, may strengthen the feeling or urge to laugh. Watch for these problems if you constantly hold back your feelings. If you have suppressed an emotional outburst of anger and you notice that the feelings of anger still rage inside of you, you may need to vent your anger privately. The person who can suppress a moment''s anger may prevent a day of sorrow.

Practice different approaches to express your anger to see how they work. Almost anything is better than destructive aggression. Always use your problem solving skills first. If you are a yeller and screamer, try quiet tolerance and daily meditation. If you are a psychological name-caller, try to use "I" statements, like "I am feeling very angry right now," or "I don't want to talk right now". If you sulk and withdraw for hours, try saying, ""I have a problem I'd like to talk about soon." If you tend to strike out with your fists, try hitting a punching bag until you can plan a reasonable verbal approach to solving the problem. Biaggio, showed that several responses are incompatible with getting intensely angry. These responses seem to help us calm down. Such responses include empathy responding, giving the offender a gift, asking for sympathy, and responding with humor. Other constructive reactions are to ask the offensive critic to clarify his/her insult or to volunteer to work with and help out the irritating person. This only works if your kindness is genuine and your offer is honest.

In addition to incompatible overt responses, there are many covert or internal responses you might use that will help suppress or control your anger. Examples: self-instructions, such as "they are just trying to make you mad" and "don't lose control and start yelling," greatly influence your view of the situation and can be very helpful in avoiding and controlling aggression. Indeed, some of the major

3

methods of anger control we use in our Anger Management groups are: Relaxation, Rational-Emotive techniques, Self-talk, Self-instructions and Stress-reduction method.

Stop hostile fantasies. Preoccupation with the irritating situation, including repeatedly talking about it, may only increase your anger. Instead try thought stopping to punish your anger-generating fantasies or substitute rewarding constructive how-to-improve-the-situation thoughts, like those suggested by Lawrence James: "I am too busy with my desire to hate as I am absorbed in something bigger than myself," or the phrase, "I have no time to quarrel, no time for regrets, and no man can force me to stoop low enough to hate him".

Guard against escalating violence. When we are mad, we frequently attempt to over-exaggerate in order to hurt the person who hurt us. There are two problems with retaliating excessively: the enemy is tempted to counterattack you even more vigorously and you will probably start thinking of the enemy even more negatively (in order to convince yourself that he/she deserved the severe punishment you gave him/her) which makes you want to aggress again. Thus, the saying, "violence breeds violence" is true. Violence produces more hate in your opponent and in you. Research has shown that controlled, moderate retaliation so that "things are equal" (in contrast to "teaching them a lesson") feels better in the long run than excessive retaliation. Better yet, it is best to walk away from the argument and let them have the last word.

Record the antecedents and consequences of your anger. As with all behaviors, you need to know the learning history of your angry reactions behavior, and what happened before and after you became angry. Your approach to others is likely to change the other person's behavior, which means you can express yourself in a way so they can understand your point of view and want to cooperate with you.

Sometimes it is best to "bite your lip" and "hold your tongue" in order to help you vent your anger privately, or to forget about it. You will be surprised how often the suppression of hot, vile, cutting remarks avoids a nasty scene. Both prevention-of-anger and control-of-anger methods are given in this section. Learn to reduce your frustrations. You know who makes you mad, what topics of conversation upset you, and the situations that drive you up a wall. Try to avoid them as this will be the best way to prevent anger. Even if you can't permanently avoid a person whom you currently dislike, staying away from that person for a few days could reduce the anger.

You may need to clarify or change your goals. Having no goals can be uncomfortable. Having impossible goals can be infuriating. You may need to plan ways to surmount the barriers that stand in your way. Learn to reduce the environmental support for your aggression. How aggressive, mean, and nasty we are is partly determined by the behavior of those around us. Perhaps you can avoid subcultures of violence, such as gangs or friends who are hostile, TV violence, or action movies. More importantly, select as your friends people who are not quick tempered or cruel and not agitators or prejudiced. Examples: if you are in high school and see your friends being very disrespectful and belligerent with teachers or parents, you are more likely to become the same way. So, choose your friends carefully. Pleasant, tactful role models as friends are very important

Explain yourself and understand others. This can make a big difference in the other person's understanding of you. One study showed that a brief comment like "I am uptight" prior to being abrasive and rude is enough to take the sting out of your aggressiveness. So, if you are getting irritated at someone for being inconsiderate of you, ask them if something is wrong, or say, "I'm sorry you are having a hard time." Similarly, if you are having a bad day and feeling grouchy, ask others (in advance) to excuse you because you are upset. This can change the environment for both you and the other person.

Develop better ways of behaving. Although you may feel like hitting the other person and cursing them out, using our most degrading and vile language, we usually realize this would be unwise.

5

Research confirms that calmly expressed anger is far more under-standable and tolerable than an emotional tirade.

MYTHS ABOUT ANGER
Myth: Anger is instinctive.
Reality: As a response, anger is primarily a learned behavior exhib-ited by those who have been able to get away with doing so. Re-sponses to anger-provoking situations are typically more learned than instinctive responses.

Myth: Activities like punching a pillow help to get rid of angry feelings.
Reality: Research shows that aggression usually inflames rather than releases anger. A person hitting a pillow as a response to an angering situation is likely to feel *angrier* after doing so than they were before hitting it. In addition, new research on anger is beginning to suggest that we have a much more complicated problem with managing our anger than the model of either keeping it in or letting it out. One group of researchers observed six distinct ways of coping with anger: direct anger-out, assertion, support-seeking, diffusion, avoidance, and rumination

Myth: Expressing anger is healthy.
Reality: Getting accustomed to expressing anger may actually es-tablish a pattern of such expression. Research findings appear to in-dicate that being chronically angry or hostile is bad for the heart. Several studies have revealed that intense anger and hostility are as-sociated with heart-related problems, including an increased risk of coronary heart disease, hypertension, blood pressure and mortality. There are mitigating factors, however: which is good news for any-one struggling to change patterns of chronic hostility. It appears that a strong social-support network, and even pet ownership, can some-what protect an individual from the negative health effects of chronic anger.

A recent study in the *International Journal of Behavioral Medi-cine* (Vol. 6, No. 3) found that those who learned to cope with anger constructively had lower resting blood pressure than those with fewer coping skills.

Myth: Men get mad, women get depressed.

Reality: Both men and women get angry with equal intensity and frequency, and for similar reasons. Men are more likely to express anger through aggressive responses, while women reportedly use a wider range of anger-coping styles, especially social support-seeking and anger-diffusion strategies. Women tend to rate their emotional distress as more intense than men, and with the exception of middle-aged and older adults, report that they experience distress for a longer duration than men.

Myth: Anger has a protective function.

Reality: Not necessarily. There's a way in which anger actually connects you to people you don't like, while it simultaneously alienates you from those you do. And displays of anger don't necessarily cause others to think that you're powerful or in control of a situation either; anger can just as easily be regarded as proof of being out of control as it can be used for the opposite view.

Often when we are angry, one or more of these emotions are going on:
1. We want something and are not getting it.
2. From past experience, we expect trouble.
3. We feel powerless to get what we want.
4. We feel sadness
5. Feelings of grief, that takes away our joy and feelings of being alive.
6. Depression.
7. Feelings of negativity about life, self, and people.

Always assume responsibility for what you are feeling, and own all your feelings, including anger. Unresolved anger turns into resentment, envy, jealousy, revenge, and hatred. There is always an underlying feeling of inadequacy when you are angry.

Anger moves through the following stages if it is not resolved immediately:

Frustration→ Over Unmet Needs Disappointment→ Embarrassment→ Guilt→ Fear of Rejection

1. **Frustration** — unfulfilled expectations. To prevent anger, change your goal or plan.
2. **Unmet Needs/Disappointment** — Your unfulfilled expectations. To prevent anger, look into situation, get the facts.
3. **Embarrassment** — expected self-image unfulfilled. The solution is tocreate new self-image.
4. **Guilt** — social expectations you have accepted. The solution is to confront the situation behavior or change it.
5. **Fear of rejection** — unknown expectations with probability of consequence. The solution is to confront the situation/person/ behavior, explore the cause then decide if you want to avoid the behavior that causes the problem.

WARNING SIGNS OF ANGER

The premise of anger management techniques is for you to use your anger as a signal to identify your problem and deal with it. Rather than act upon your anger by lashing out, to make the situation worse, or to hold your angry feelings inside.

Anger can lead to:

1. Angrily Lashing out→ makes the situation worse holding inside→ Create resentment, physical symptoms

OR

You can identify the problem to handle or solve it. You do this by changing your thoughts. This is helpful when thinking about something that irritates you and makes you mad.

When a situation provokes you and you are preparing to respond, begin thinking and ask yourself some critical questions.

1. How can I manage this situation?
2. What is it that I absolutely have to do?
3. Decide how you will regulate your anger?
4. Will an argument between you and the other person solve your problem?
5. Do you have a plan for time to calm down or relax when angry?

ALTERNATIVES TO ANGRILY ACTING OUT

Rethink, to change your expression of anger, you must change your thinking

Change what you say to yourself, in response to the external event.

1. Take time to rethink about what has provoked you.
2. Use a planned relaxation technique
3. Stay calm and keep your cool
4. Ask yourself if you are overreacting, taking things too seriously, or justifying your right to be angry.

PURPOSE OF YOUR ANGER WORK-OUT

This will familiarize you with three essential emotional components of anger. They are your:

1. Thoughts
2. Words
3. Behavior

TRIGGERS OF ANGER
Major Causes of Anger Are:

1. Grief — Loss-Past/Present/Future
2. Sadness→ Hurt→ Emotional Pain
3. Resentment→ Envy→ Hate
4. Victim Mind Set — Lack of boundaries for you
5. Abuse — a) Deep dependency needs, b) Revenge

6. Low Self-Esteem — a) Jealousy, b) Envy
7. Fear — of the Unknown/of Rejection
8. Unmet Needs — a) Lack of nurturance, b) Low self-worth
9. Unfulfilled Expectations about love/life —Loneliness.

SECONDARY CAUSES OF ANGER
1. Stress
2. Desire to have or be in control of things
3. Intolerance to criticism
4. Chronic deficit of attention or recognition
5. Feelings of abandonment
6. Feelings of rejection
7. Fragile emotions/low ego strength (inability to recognize or accept one's faults)
8. Antagonistic/Argumentative disposition
9. Narcissistic/Self-centered
10. Superiority/Inferiority complex — A "Be Perfect Script".

"We Are the Ones We Have Been Waiting For"

Effective communication puts the burden on the sender to ensure that the understanding and meaning of the intended message is delivered. Do you expect others to read your mind and try to figure out what you intend to say? Do you follow up on faulty or misunderstood communication or do you assume the worst? Write your response below.

ANGER MANAGEMENT BASIC CONCEPTS TO UNDERSTAND

To change your expression of anger, you must change your thinking. **Rethink**. Change what you say to yourself, in response to the external event.

1. Anger is a powerful emotion
2. Reason is not employed when we are angry
3. Anger is the result of jumping to conclusions about an outcome
4. Anger creates energy, excitement and negative "aliveness"
5. Anger is self-serving
6. Anger is addictive/obsessive thinking you can't let go.
7. Anger is about power and control
8. Anger is used to intimidate, instill fear, and as an outlet to get rid of one's inner poison/toxins
9. You do not have a license to hurt or abuse another person with your anger
10. No one has given you permission to hurt them, because of your inability to handle your problems
11. When you are angry, you are out of control, not the other person
12. Others may provoke you to anger, but you do not have to respond angrily. When you respond as others want, they have the power to control you
13. No one is the cause of you responding angrily. You have freedom of choice
14. When you get mad, you are exercising your power to avenge yourself
15. You get some pleasure from hurting others, if you get angry repeatedly
16. If you get angry repeatedly, you are unable to control your destructive urges and feel the need to get even
17. Anger is a powerful emotion, either you control it, or you are controlled by it.

Draw a picture of your anger.

A Definition of Anger

Everybody has his or her own definition of anger. *Webster's New World Dictionary* defines it as a noun, meaning a feeling of displeasure, resulting from injury, mistreatment, opposition, which shows itself as a desire to fight back at the person, situation or event they feel caused the feeling to occur.

We define anger as:

- ·An emotion, that is physically arousing with unique physiological correlates.
- A feeling. It has an effect on the way you experience your world.
- A communicator. Anger sends information to others.
- A cause. Anger produces specific effects and results.

Think about your definition of *anger* and write your thoughts below.

Descriptive words to better understand who you are:

1.
2.
3.
4.

Anger Is A Signal

Anger is a valuable signal, because it lets us know when something is wrong and needs to be corrected. The critical factor is whether your expression of anger is adding to the problem rather than solving your problem.

Often when we are angry, one or more of these things are going on:

1. We have learned to respond in an angry manner
2. We have become conditioned and maybe addicted to feeling the energy which is anger
3. We feel powerless to get what we want.

The premise of anger management techniques is for you to use your anger as a signal to identify your problem and deal with it, rather than act upon your anger by lashing out, to make the situation worse, or to hold your angry feelings inside.

ANGER MANAGEMENT ASSESSMENT

1. Are your feelings about anger good or bad?

2. Describe your bodily reactions when you get angry: e.g. I feel tightness in my throat:

3. In what part of your body (muscle group) do you feel the emotion of anger mostly? Shoulders, face, jaws, hands tremble etc.

4. Are you able to think about your body reactions when you are angry?

5. Are you able to think about what caused you to get/be angry, when you are angry? **Write about this**.

5. What do you feel when you are angry? Select from the list below and explain why you selected it.
   a) Out of control
   b) Powerful
   c) Powerless

Methods for Handling Our Anger and Aggression

The adages of "count to 10" or "engage brain before starting mouth" are probably good ideas. Do whatever you can to stop your impulsive aggression, like hitting or yelling. Even a brief delay may permit you to think of a more constructive response. Actually the longer the delay the better, perhaps sleep on it or talk to a friend first. Research with children has confirmed Seneca's opinion that thinking about other things helps reduce our frustration (Seneca was a Roman philosopher, who lived about 2000 years ago). Do something you enjoy, something that occupies your mind. Listen to music, take a bath, meditate, watch a comic movie, or use a little comedy if you can control the sarcasm.

Exercises to Identify Anger

1. Write your definition of extreme frustration or anger. Is anger a good or bad feeling for you to express?

2. Are you able to think about your body reactions when you are angry?

3. Are you able to think about what caused you to get/be angry, when you are angry?

4. How soon after your expression of anger, can you relax?

5. What do you feel when you are angry and why?
   a) Good
   b) Sad
   c) Guilty
6. Conflict is sometimes unavoidable when you are angry. What is your method to handle conflict?

Anger Management Coping Statements

Try using some of these statements the next time you feel yourself getting angry, or make up your own. Circle the ones you think will work best.

1. Stay calm. Just relax.
2. As long as I keep my cool, I am in control.
3. Just roll with the punches; don't get bent out of shape.
4. Think of what you want to get out of this.
5. You don't need to prove yourself to anyone.
6. There's no point in getting mad.
7. Look for the positives.
8. I'm not going to let this get to me.
9. It is a shame she/he has to act like this.
10. He's probably really unhappy if he's acting that irritable.
11. What she/he says doesn't matter.
12. I can't expect people to act the way I want them to all the time.
13. My muscles feel tight; it is time to relax.
14. He'd probably like me to fly off the handle. Well, he's going to be disappointed.

15. Let's work this problem out. Maybe he/she has a point.
16. I'm not going to be pushed around, but I'm not going to lose it either.
17. I'm in control. I can handle this.
18. I have a right to be annoyed, but I want to reason this out.
19. Slow down and take a few deep breaths.
20. Try to reason it out. Let's treat each other with respect.

LEARNING HOW TO MONITOR AND TRACK YOUR FEELINGS OF ANGER

ch Choose one behavior from the following list, making sure the one you ch1oose is not something you want to change. (Your goal is to practice watching yourself, not to change your behavior.) Next to the behavior you choose, write how you will measure it (frequency or interval).

Feelings of anger

_____

_____

Making telephone calls

_____

_____

Watching television

_____

_____

Self-monitor your behavior for five days. At the end of each day, transfer your data into a graph grid already prepared.

Number of times

OR
Averagelength of time
the behavior occurred

5

4

3

2

1

Days   1   2   3   4   5

NOW TAKE ACTION

After you have practiced self-monitoring, begin to self-monitor the frequency of your anger for seven days (the longer, the better). Measure your data by moving pennies, or toothpicks from one pocket to another, or use some other way that is convenient for you. To make it easier for you, here are your daily data sheet and graph grid.

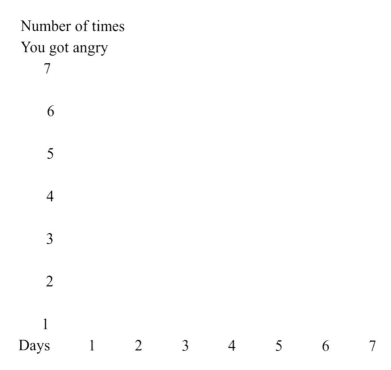

Number of times
You got angry

7

6

5

4

3

2

1

Days   1   2   3   4   5   6   7

THE NINE TRUTHS ABOUT VIOLENCE

We are all 100% for our own behavior.

Violence is not an acceptable solution to problems.

We do not have control over any person, but we do have control over ourselves.

When communicating with someone else, we need to express our feelings directly rather than blaming or threatening.

Increased awareness of self-talk, physical cues and emotions is essential for progress and improvement.

We can always take a time-out before reacting.

We can't do anything about the past, but we can change the future.

Although there are differences between men and women, our needs and rights are fundamentally alike.

Counselors and case managers cannot make people change — they can only set the stage for change to occur.

OUR THOUGHTS AFFECT OUR ANGER

Many types of thoughts affect anger, but the most important ones come from a type of thinking process called cognitive appraisal. This is the mental process that helps us define and interpret what is happening to or around us. Its roots lie in special qualities and circumstances — family background, natural talents, physical appearances, and systems of belief — that helps us shape our personalities. These combine to form the basis for the unique way each of us appraises the situations we encounter in daily life.

The way we appraise our environment at any given moment is crucial in determining how we respond emotionally. While this thought is not original, Epictetus,a Greek philosopher, said, two thousand years ago, "Men are not troubled by things themselves, but by their thoughts about them." Today, psychologists agree that it is the meaning we assign to events that gives them the power to affect us for good or ill. Here are some facts about cognitive appraisal as they relate to working out anger:

The cognitive activity (thinking) in appraisal does not imply anything about deliberate reflection, rationality, or awareness. When we are angry, the appraisals that we make are frequently distorted, influencing us to act in what appears to others a highly irrational way. "He got out of control," we say. "He wasn't thinking. If he had been, he wouldn't have acted that way." But he was thinking. In other words, the process of appraisal — independent of how it is used — is continually in use, and you are continually using it.

The workout process takes advantage of the appraisal process by improving your appraisal skills so that you can use them to assess, manage, and strategically direct anger for productive gains. "I didn't understand" is one of the most costly sentences in modern business. Breakdowns in dialogue cause much of the expensive dissention, indecision, and wrong decision-making in business. Would you guess that approximately 90 percentof all job failures are due to a lack of technical skills? It is much the same with communication in relationships.

20

Anger is triggered by external events called provocations. These create angry thoughts, arousal, and angry actions, which escalate each other until they are fused together like the three prongs on a pitchfork, in an anger feedback loop that leads to destructive consequences. The more intense the anger, the harder it is to break The feedback loop. As the center of the triangle (thoughts, arousal, action) gets smaller, the tension or fusion increases, making productive actions or change harder to generate. Productive actions cannot be made when the anger feedback loop is completely fused. When we work through our anger, it prevents total fusions.

HOW EMOTIONAL ANGER WORKS
   a) **Provocation** — behaviors that stimulate angry thoughts or arousal.
   b) **Action** — your response to an unmet need; created by your expectations of what the outcome will be.
   c) **Angry Feelings** — feelings you justify as right for you to express.

How Dialogue Can Help You?
These are the payoffs to the person learning and using the skills of effective communication.

Dialogue is a way to:
   1. Unleash the creative thinking of all-employees, associates, customers, and ourselves.
   2. Create a more comfortable working environment...
   3. Increase understanding and decrease job turnover.
   4. Establish a fertile atmosphere for self-motivation.
   5. Stimulate and sustain interpersonal relationships.
   6. Implement participative management.
   7. Uncover problems and discover causes.
   8. Clarify and verify responsibilities and relationships.
   9. Calm tempers
   10. Chart a joint course of action for all concerned parties.

THE ENERGY FLOW AND BEHAVIOR PROGRESSION OF ANGER
Feelings Checklist on Anger

Low	Medium	High
Irritated	Mad	Enraged
Bugged	Pissed	Furious
Disturbed	Ticked	Hateful
Annoyed	Disgusted	Vicious
Bothered	Offended	Indignant
Cross	Irked	Adamant
Upset	Frustrated	Infuriated

Sadness	Fear
Dejected	Afraid
Depressed	Frightened
Melancholy	Timid, Abandoned
Shy	Guilty
Powerless, Hopeless	Desperate,
Gloomy	Impatient
Lonely	Suspicious
Heartbroken	Dubious
Disappointed	Hesitant,
Envious	Nervous
Embarrassed	Horrified
Dismal	Scared

Chapter 2

Healthy Relationship Communication

There are some specific skills that you can learn to use to improve communication with another person. The optimal way to improve communication in a relationship is for both partners to learn and practice the skills together. But even if your partner doesn't happen to be learning with you right now, one person using these skills can have an impact on a relationship.

This approach to communication is based upon the following three assumptions. The **first** basic assumption is that feeling, all kinds, **exist** They are both neither good nor bad, wrong nor right, correct nor incorrect — they just **are**. The **second** assumption is that all of us have the **right** to have any feeling in the world. Some **behaviors** or actions may need to be limited, but **any feeling** is okay. And each one of us is the **ultimate authority** on our own feelings. **No one** can tell you what you do or don't feel. Another person may not like what you are feeling or may feel differently. But no one can tell you that you don't feel the way you do. The **third** assumption is that an intimate relationship, at its best, is a place where both partners feel safe to share feeling, when they choose to, without getting attacked for doing so.

In effective communication, there are two sets of skills. One set is for listening, and the other is for speaking. Both are essential.

Skills for Listening

Have you ever heard a conversation like this?

Her: Blah, Blah.

Him: Yak, Yak.

Her: What I said was blah, blah.

Him: What I said was yak, yak.

Her: But don't you see that I am saying, blah, blah?

Him: You won't even recognize that I have already said yak, yak.
Her: How blind can you be?
Him: Who's blind around here?

You can fill in the words of the "blah, blah" or the "yak, yak" with anything you like. The point is that each person continues re-stating his or her own position. Each partner may be expressing important feelings, but their words will go to waste unless they listen, really hear, and validate each other. Validation means that you communicate to your partner that, if you were seeing things his or her way, standing on his or her platform, with his or her assumptions about things, that it would make sense and be reasonable to feel that way. You are not saying, "I agree with you," or "You are right, and I am wrong." You are just admitting the possibility that another point of view may make sense.

How to Validate or Use Active Listening:
Listen to your partner. What is the content? What is the feeling?
Be aware of any "hidden agendas" that might be functioning as "filters" through which you are hearing your partner"s message. For instance, if "being criticized" is an issue for you, you may "hear" more criticism than is actually present.
Paraphrase, in your own words, both content and feelings. You have to get into your partner's shoes and experience the feeling, and then let your partner know that you hear the message. This can be hard to do, especially when you feel hurt and not listened to, but it is a crucial and valuable skill.

Don'ts and Do's for Effective Listening:
Don't say or imply that your partner "shouldn't feel that way."
Don't express your feelings — of disagreement or agreement — or make suggestions at this point.
Don't interpret out loud what you think your partner "really feels.'
Don't try to get your partner to change his or her mind.

24

Do remember that every person has the right to any feeling in the world.

Do put your own feelings "on a back burner" while you are the "listener.'

Later, when you are the speaker, you will have a chance to express your feelings, and your partner will listen to you.

Here Are Some Examples of Active Listening:

"Sounds like you want it too, but are worried about how we'll be able to pay for it."

'What I'm hearing you say is that my not checking with you first caused you a lot of embarrassment."

'Your first choice is to go out for pizza, second choice is to grill hamburgers at home, and you really don't want to go out for chicken. Did I get that right?"

"Let me check out if I'm hearing you accurately. What you minded wasn"t so much that the house was dirty, but you felt that I didn't care enough to clean it."

"You're saying you really like it when we snuggle up on the sofa."

Skills For Speaking

Use I-messages. An I-message is a sentence that starts with the word "I" and expresses a feeling. Here is why an "I-message" is more effective than a "you-message." Suppose X says to Y, 'You play too much golf.' Y can protest, "I do not." Y feels attacked and put down and is tempted to retaliate with a counterattack. But if X says to Y, "I feel jealous when you play golf," Y cannot say "you do not." X is taking responsibility for his or her own feelings, and no one can say that X doesn't or shouldn't feel that way.

To communicate what you are feeling, you need to know what you are feeling. This takes practice. It involves getting to know you body and the signals it gives to tell you what you are feeling. It also

25

involves becoming familiar with the typical pattern of thoughts that go along with specific feelings for you. To help you start this process, use the sample feeling chart below. When you want to know what you are feeling, you might look at the chart and select the word that best approximates how you feel at the moment.

I feel: 1. A little   2. Somewhat   3. Very

Positive:

relaxed	willing	content	turned on
calm	secure	loving	Interest
warm	strong	bubbly	ambitious
sexy	happy	peaceful	imaginative
excited	busy	confident	close to you

Negative:

grouchy	ashamed	silly	sorry
sad	bored	hurt	incompetent
anxious	alone	shy	rebellious
tired	dumb	guilty	confused
nervous-	trapped	frustrated	listless
restless	put down	depressed	uninterested

When you speak in I-statements, you don't have to use complicated feeling words. Someone once said that there are four basic feelings and three of them rhyme: mad, sad, glad and afraid. If you're ever not sure what you're feeling, scan through those four.

1. Mad
2. Sad
3. Glad
4. Afraid/Fear

Other useful feeling words are:
1. I like it when…
2. I don't like it when…
3. I want….
4. I wish…

Sometimes our feelings have two parts: for example, I want to go, but I don't want to spend the money. That is a perfectly legitimate I-statement, so when you feel two things, say both of them.

Other Don'ts and Do's for Effective Speaking:

Don't ask questions.

Don't judge, preach, criticize, or blame.

Don't use name calling.

Don't interpret, diagnose, or analyze.

Do "own" your feeling. For example, "I get mad."

Do be specific when you feel that way. For example, "I get mad when clothes are on the bathroom floor."

Do say directly what you want. For example, "I would like you to take them out of the bathroom."

Here is a formula you can use to build an I-message when you want to give your partner feedback about his or her behavior.

"When you do … X (describe the behavior), I feel … Y."

And if you want change, add:

"I'd prefer … Z." (describe the behavior).

Here are some examples of effective speaking:

"I really appreciated your calling me this afternoon."

"I felt confused and surprised when the car was there instead of the truck. I didn't know whether to be mad at you or angry with myself for getting my signals crossed."

"I'm sort of hesitant to bring this up, because I know we've gotten into an argument about this before, but I really want to talk about my sister and the kids before we go over there tonight."

GUIDELINES FOR SPEAKING AND LISTENING

To express a positive feeling or appreciation:

Speaker:	**Listener:**
"I like it when …"	"You liked it when …"

To express a negative feeling, concern, or request for changes:

Speaker:	**Listener:**
"I didn't like when …"	"You didn't like it when …"
or	or
"I'd prefer …"	"You'd rather that …"

This formula gives you a format to use to start your sentences if you are not sure how to begin as speaker or listener. Remember, when you are the listener, your goal is not to parrot back what the speaker said. Your goal is to understand what the speaker was feeling, and let him or her know that you understand. Here is a listening and speaking exercise you can practice with a partner.

IMPROVE YOUR LISTENING SKILLS EXERCISE

Name   ....

Hear the implicit I-statement in someone's message, especially if the person is not speaking clearly for you to understand. Evaluate the following statements:

"You are accusing me."
I think he is saying I am judging him, when I say these words or my tone of voice says it.

"Get out of here!"
I think he's mad, and getting madder by the minute.
He doesn't want to deal with me at all right now.
He wants to be alone.

"If you loved me, you'd ...
It sounds like she wants this badly
It must feel to her like I don't love her when I tell her I don't want her to go.

Some Ways To Prevent Violence

1. We are all 100% responsible for our own behavior.
2. Violence is not an acceptable solution to problems.
3. We do not have control over any person, but we do have control over ourselves.
4. When communicating with someone else, we need to express our feelings directly rather than blaming or threatening.
5. Increasing awareness of self-talk, physical cues, and emotions is essential for progress and improvement.
6. We can always take a time-out before reacting.
7. We can't do anything about the past, but we can change the future.
8. Although there are differences between men and women, our needs and rights are fundamentally alike.
9. Counselors and other professionals cannot make people change — they can only set the stage for change to occur.

WHAT IS ASSERTIVENESS?

Assertiveness is the ability to clearly state what you want (or don't want) and feel, without trampling on the rights of others in the process. The whole question of "rights" is what causes people such a problem. In order to assert yourself, you need to keep in mind your rights and the rights of others. We often become confused about what we have the right to do, and what we don't. Here are some generally accepted guidelines that you can keep in mind.

Non-Assertive People

We all attempt to have our needs met one way or another. For those who are unable to be assertive, there are basically three alternatives – none of which is very successful: the aggressive approach, the passive approach, and the passive-aggressive approach.

Aggression

Sometimes people confuse assertiveness with aggressive behavior. Although there is a fine line between the two, it is an important distinction to make. The assertive individual lets others know what is on his or her mind: "It's been a long day and I'm beat — I don't feel like cooking. I'd like to go out to eat tonight. How about you?" The aggressive person is more likely to say, "You never cook! You don't have any idea what it's like to come home day after day and prepare dinner after a long day at work. I'm sick and tired of it. You can take me out or fix your own dinner!" In the dialogue, the first person expresses how she's feeling and what she'd like to do about it. An aggressive person blames, demands, and bullies the other.

Aggressive behavior does have its place. In business, for instance, aggressive marketing or sales is often a plus. But when it comes to personal relationships (those between family members, friends, neighbors, or colleagues), the overly aggressive individual eventually drives others away. This is usually the last thing he or she wanted to do.

Passivity

"If you can't say something nice, don't say anything at all." Being nice, pleasant, avoiding conflict is a lesson many people, especially women, have had drilled into them from an early age. Another word for striving to be constantly nice and undemanding is *passive.*

Passive people are the proverbial doormats: they allow people to walk all over them and they never make a fuss. They are the ones who routinely say "I don't care," "whatever you want," or "it's up to you."

The problem with passivity is that it leads to a lot of anger and confusion. The passive person becomes angry because he isn't getting what he wants, while others become frustrated and confused because they don't know what he wants. A conversation with a passive person might go something like this:

31

"Let's go out. What do you like doing?"
"Anything — I don't really care, whatever you want to do."
"How about a movie?"
"Sure."
"Anything special you want to see?"
"No, anything is fine."
"How about Texas Chainsaw Massacre 14?"
"If you want to."
"Great, let's go."
But then later:
"You know I hate violent movies! Why can't we ever do anything I want to do?"

In this case, the lack of assertion causes trouble between the two people. The assertive person might have responded, "Almost any movie's fine as long as it's not one of those stupid horror movies. I really dislike all the violence in them." Or, " I don't know about a movie. How about that new play?" And an assertive response might be, "I'm not crazy about plays. Want to go to the comedy club?"

Nice guys, if they're too nice, do finish last. They don't end up getting what they want, they feel unreasonably used and abused, and they drive everyone else crazy in the process.

Passive-Aggressive

This is a psychological term which means expressing hostility, anger, or resentment in a passive (indirect) way — usually in response to a request or demand that someone else has made. Passive-aggressive people seem compliant; they rarely raise their voices, disagree, or even express strong opinions. When asked to do something, they may readily agree, but then not do it. Even though passive-aggressive people rarely show anger, they often infuriate those around them.

Fear of Rejection

"I can't ask for a raise: what if she says no?" When people say "no" to you, does it make you feel as if they're rejecting you as a person? Usually, it simply means that your request has been denied — not that they think you are a worthless individual. But if, deep down, you have serious self-doubts about how lovable or capable you are, you may interpret "no" as confirmation of what you've suspected all along: you're not worth much. This is extremely unlikely! When asking for a raise, make a list of the skills you've developed, the tasks you are responsible for, the objectives you've achieved. Lay these out when you make your request. If it's denied, you need to ask for an explanation — the reason may have nothing to do with the work you are doing, but with the company's financial position at the present time.

The Need to Be "Liked"

"I really don't have the energy or the time to watch her children after school this week, but if I refuse, she'll be really ticked at me." Do you believe that people like you only if you do things for them? Is fulfilling others' needs the only way to get and keep friends? Friendship, like any other close relationship, should be a give-and-take proposition. The person who likes you only if you meet her needs — while never asking how she might meet yours — is selfish and is using you. This is an unhealthy relationship, not a friendship.

How would an assertive person act in this situation? By explaining that this isn't a good week for you to watch her kids, and that you hope she'll be able to make other arrangements. A true friend will appreciate the help you've given in the past, respect you for speaking up, and not "hold it against you."

FEAR OF CONFLICT

"I just know if I tell him I need to change my work hours, it's going to lead to a big fight; it's not worth it."

Changes rarely occur without some amount of conflict. However, conflict doesn't have to lead to a major battle. How you present a request will largely determine the response your request gets.

An aggressive approach ("This schedule is lousy, and I'm not doing it anymore") is likely to lead to a battle and won't get you what you want. The passive approach ("Sometime, maybe, I'd like to change my schedule") won't cause conflict; it'll just be ignored. The assertive approach ("Some things have come up in my personal life so that I'll need to rearrange my schedule. When can we talk about this?") will work best. There will be some conflict as compromises are made; but odds are, even if you don't get exactly what you want, your schedule will work better than it did before.

"Assertive" and "Selfish" — They Are Not the Same

"I can't ask her to help me with my work when she has her own work to do. That would be selfish."

Expressing your needs, asking for (and even expecting) help is not selfish. Your needs are valid. It may or may not be possible to meet them, but you certainly have a right to make them known — again, in a direct, non-accusatory way. Selfishness means caring only about your own needs and desires. Assertiveness means meeting those needs and desires *while thinking of others as well.*

How to Handle Feelings of Guilt

Do you feel uncomfortable asking for help? Do you think that if you do need help, it's because you're incompetent? Do you think that you're dependent, demanding, or unreasonable if you ask for help?

Pushing Buttons

People who are unable to stand up for themselves are easy to push around. Expert manipulators know which of your buttons to push to stir up feelings of guilt, rejection, anxiety, or fear. And once those buttons have been pushed, the unassertive person will quickly back down and give in.

Can you avoid being a pushover? These tips can help you to know when your buttons are being pushed and how to respond:

Identify your personal fears or weaknesses. For instance, is it impossible for you to remain assertive if someone gets emotional every time you make a request? Or, do you back right down if someone implies that you're being selfish?

Acknowledge how you feel when, after acting assertively, you are met with resistance. For example, let's say your in-laws have invited you to spend your summer vacation with them, but you've already made other plans. After thanking them and explaining why you won't be able to visit, they sigh and say, "That's okay; this is what happens when you get old. People have no time for you anymore."

How to Stand Up for Yourself!

Keep your statements or requests short and to the point. *Don't* ramble. If you need a day off, say so. Don't say, "I was trying to get a dental appointment, and now one opened up, so …"

Don't say "maybe" when you mean "no." It's not honest; it's wishy-washy; and it leaves the door open for argument.

Don't say "I don't care" when you do. Often the I-don't-care response is a way of not taking responsibility for making a decision. Or, it may be a way if saying, "It's up to you, but if you really care for me you'll know what I want." No one can read your mind. If you want something known, speak up.

Don't phrase expectations as a question. Better to say, "Please clean up your room before dinner," than "Do you think you can get your room cleaned up before dinner?" Phrasing is like taxes: if people can find a loophole, they'll usually use it!

Be specific — don't generalize. If you'd like some help driving the children around after school say so: "Can you pick Tom up from baseball practice a Wednesday?" Avoid "It seems like I spend all my time in the car. I wish I had some help."

Don't turn your statement or opinion into a question. "I thought it was a really good movie, didn't you?" It sounds like you're uncertain and waiting for the other person to affirm what you said.

Use "I" statements. "I'd like you to cook tonight" is more direct than, 'You haven't cooked for a while."

Take responsibility for what you say. "I disagree" sounds stronger and more mature than "No one agrees with you."

Direct your statements to the person it's intended for. Rather than complaining to coworkers about how unfair your boss has been to you, tell your boss.

THE POWER OF NON-VERBAL MESSAGES

- **Maintain eye contact** — but don't stare. When you allow your gaze to wander around the room (or be fixed on your feet) you lose contact. You're likely to lose the thread of the conversation, too, and others will wonder exactly what point you're trying to make. Staring, on the other hand, makes others uncomfortable. The best approach is to focus on the other person's face and occasionally look them in the eye.
- **Don't loom or cower.** As much as possible, try to mirror the other person's stance, so that you both seem more equal. If he's standing, stand up and face him. If he's sitting, take a seat facing him. Standing over people and talking down to them can be intimidating. Conversely, sinking into a sofa while trying to make a point (to someone who is standing) gives an impression of inferiority or helplessness. Even when you're talking on the phone, it's best to stand or sit up straight. You will feel more confident and behave more assertively.
- **Keep your facial expressions consistent with what you are saying.** Smiling can be a major problem here. Many people smile when delivering a message they fear will upset or anger the other

person; smiling is a way of saying, "Look, I'm being nice, don't get mad." Some people smile when they're angry, either because they don't recognize their own anger or because they're uncomfortable being seen as angry. Smiling is a way of trying to please others even when you're delivering unpleasant news. Smiling at such times indicates that you're uncomfortable with your message; it's confusing to others.

ASSERTIVENESS IS A "TWO-WAY STREET"

- Learn to listen carefully. Don't interrupt or try to come up with a reply before the other person has finished speaking. That's a defensive approach, not an assertive one.

- Learn to be diplomatic. Tailor your style to the situation. Some people respond well to humor (which is not the same as ridicule or sarcasm), while others are more comfortable just hearing the facts.

- Ask for clarification. Make sure you understand what's being said before you respond. If your child's teacher simply asks for help in the classroom, you don't have enough information to say "yes" or "no". How often? What time? For a few weeks or for the whole school year? You have a right to ask for clarification, and you have the obligation to provide clarification when others ask it from you.

SENDING A MESSAGE "DO AS I DO"

The self-confident child is one who feels she has the same rights that adults have. She has a right to ask for things, a right to say "no" a right to change her mind, and a right to her own opinions and values. And she needs to know, as you do, that having rights doesn't mean she'll always get her way.

- Help her distinguish between those things she has a right refuse and those1 she doesn't. Politely refusing an invitation is okay; refusing to go to school is not.

- Show respect for her opinions even when they conflict with yours. You can let her know that you don't agree even while accepting her right to *have* and *express* an opinion.
- Teach your child the difference between assertiveness and aggression. Pushing someone off a swing is very different from saying, "It's my turn now."
- Whining and sulking are indirect ways that children (and adults) sometimes use to express dissatisfaction. Teach her you can't respond to her if she doesn't explain herself or talk in her "regular" voice.

HOW TO ASK FOR A BEHAVIOR CHANGE
Describe
- Describe the other person's behavior objectively.
- Use concrete terms.
- Describe a specified time, place, and frequency of the action.
- Describe the action, not the "motive."

Express
- Express your feelings.
- Express them calmly.
- State feelings in a positive manner related to the goal.
- Direct yourself to the specific offending behavior, not to the whole person.

Empathize
- If possible, show some understanding of the other's position.
- Be honest, not sarcastic.

EFFECTIVE PARENTING SKILLS
Develop pride in children rather than anger and frustration.

1. **Promise:**
   a) keep your promise,
   b) do not try to manipulate out of a promise.

2. **Reflection:** reflect back what the child is doing/behaving.

3. **Imitation:** do what the child does (yell, get angry).

4. **Description:** say what the child is doing wrong.

5. **Enthusiasm:** try to be enthusiastic when the child is looking for solace or comfort.

6. **Ignoring:** ignore when they behave badly. Turn your chair away when they are behaving badly and tell them "I like you when you are behaving well."

7. **Strengthen** the relationship with the child: follow the child's lead.

8. **Words to avoid**: no, shut up, quit, and stop.

9. **State what you want them to do**, "I want you to walk down the hall."

Chapter 3

Anger the Toxic Emotion

Just as we have an outlet to exercise our body, we need an outlet to get rid of our toxic feelings. Any behavior we engage more than one time becomes a habit. Any habit we repeat more than twice becomes an ingrained behavior pattern in the brain and has the potential to become an addictive behavior. An addictive behavior is a neuronal imprint in the brain and cells that is coded data and remembered by the brain. Anger is neither good nor bad; however, our expression of it can have catastrophic consequences if others experience us in a negative manner. When you decide to change the way you express your anger it will be challenging and difficult because you have developed a way of reacting and responding to people and situations in an automatic learned manner. Old learned behaviors are not easily deleted without relearning or retraining of a new ways of responding. I refer to this new reprogramming as re-training or as an "Anger Work-out".

It is a mental work-out of the brain and nerve cells in your body. When you stop doing any of the anger "work-outs", your old counterproductive anger habits are likely to re-emerge. The more you work out, the less chance there is to be hurt by your old anger habits. Eventually, you will be able to do the "work-outs" on an automatic basis. When this happens you will be more productive in all aspects of your life. Working out your anger shapes you up mentally, physically, and spiritually.

One thing anyone can do to enhance their self-esteem is to be in control of all toxic emotions. A toxic emotion is any emotion that has the potential to cause harm to another person, create disharmony between you and another, to be a source of conflict, cause irreparable damage to a relationship, or to destroy an interaction between you and another.

40

The following are emotions I consider toxic: Envy, Jealousy, Revenge, Fear, Hatred, and Anger. All of these emotions are addressed extensively in my book, *Light the Fire Within You*. Anger will be discussed here because it is often the cause of problems between you and others.

Anger is a chosen position. We can decide how we will react to a perceived threat to our ego, or emotional comfort. Anger is a signal for you to look at what is going on in your emotions and to identify the cause of the anger.

Anger is a waste of energy. It takes away your joy. It can be used by others to confuse or control you, if you are unaware of what you are feeling, unclear about what angers you, or have no control over your anger outbursts. Anger takes away energy because it emotionally charges you, even when used constructively. Because of its potential to hurt or destroy others' self-confidence, anger must be under your control. Anger can be very destructive when uncontrolled.

Anger is useful when used to support you against abuse, even though anger is always a loss of energy. However, anger is a valuable signal because it lets us know when something is wrong and needs to be corrected. The critical factor is whether your expression of anger is adding to your problem rather than solving your problem.

When you develop inner control of a powerful emotion like anger, you become powerful. When you are controlled by your outer environment, you have lost the opportunity for inner control. To become good at any skill requires continuous practice, whether it is controlling your expression of anger, or your tongue. We each have an internal comfort zone that lets us know what we are feeling. Most of us are out of touch with our feelings and ignore our internal comfort zone temperature.

INTERNAL COMFORT ZONES

- A comfort zone is an internal regulation that alerts you to either feeling comfortable with a person or situation, or "out of place"
.
- When you feel out of place, it shuts off your recall and the • harder you try the less you remember.
- The first thing to go is your voice.
- Comfort zones are like thermostats.
- Listen to the words and assimilate; more importantly, listen to the tone of voice.
- Meaningful and lasting change will only take place if it comes from within; start with your self-image (inside), the change will then take place (outside).
- As we imprint the new, we become dissatisfied with our old self.

Old Self-Image	New Self-Image
Discomfort	Comfort Zone
Creative Subconscious	Creative Conscious Awareness

A SIMPLE ANGER-MANAGEMENT TECHNIQUE

In times of real frustration, it can be difficult to remember what day of the week it is, let alone a complex method for dealing with angry feelings. That's why the simple acronym, "**D.E.S.K.**" can be an effective method for keeping ones cool in times of heightened emotion.

D.E.S.K. comes from the assertiveness school of anger management. Assertiveness is different and distinct from aggressiveness and involves being direct about needs or setting a limit. The heart of the model, however, is about showing respect for other people's needs, feelings and rights as well.

D — Describe the behavior. If the situation involves another person, try to describe specifically what they've done or said to upset you. If the anger does not involve another person, you should still attempt to articulate what you're thinking or feeling. Writing it down or telling a friend what's going on helps to define the feelings, which can render them more manageable.

E — Express the feeling using an "I" statement. Particularly if the anger involves another person, it's important that you put your thoughts in this form. "I" statements offer a chance to put forth your own personal perspective, but also demonstrate that you realize others may have their own version of the situation. For example, saying, "I feel really frustrated with how you're handling this situation," shows more respect for the other person than a more accusatory form of the same sentiment such as, "You're handling this badly."

S — State what you need or want. What would make the situation better?

K — Know that you may not get it. Remember, the assertive model doesn't guarantee a perfect resolution, but it does provide a framework for expressing anger that offers a greater sense of control. A greater sense of control can go a long way toward mitigating stress and frustration.

Steps to Control Your Anger:

1. Make a list of the things that make you mad, and memorize it.

2. Talk about your feelings, let people knows when things bother you.

3. When you feel angry, do something with the negative energy. Slowly breathe in and out ten times. On the exhale, spread you fingers apart widely and imagine the negative energy leaving your body as you do so.

4. When you feel the urge to strike out at someone, shrug (raise) your shoulders as you breathe in deeply, and rapidly lower your shoulders as you exhale. Notice your jaw muscles, shoulders,

hands, chest, and torso muscles. Get in touch with what you are angry about, and with whom you are angry.

5. Make peace with yourself and the person who is the object of your anger. Forgive yourself first. Then apologize to the other person for your lack of control.

6. Mentally visualize two paths, (there is an exercise in my book *Light the Fire within You* that teaches you how to visualize). Have one of these paths be positive, pleasant, and full of light. Have the other path be dark, gloomy, and depressive. Then send your angry feelings down the dark path and over a cliff.

7. Notice if you feel like yelling, screaming, or hitting. Before you act on your anger, think of why you are angry. Is your angry feeling legitimate, or did you create a situation to justify your anger?

8. Talk your way through your anger. Tell yourself you can change from being a reactor of your emotions to being a processor. Notice your thoughts, change negative thoughts to positive.

9. Change the image you have of yourself from "blowing your stack," to "being a cool headed person." Whenever you are able to control your anger, reinforce it by saying something kind to yourself.

10. Daily seek ways to change your image, inner thoughts, and outer behavior, so the two match.

11. See yourself as a kind person.

12. Seek to become a thinker rather than an emotional reactor. To be an emotional reactor is to be out of control. An emotional reac-

tor is a person who discharges and wastes valuable energy needed by the brain to process information. When you are an emotional reactor you deplete your body of vital minerals and nutrients.

13. Pay attention to your feelings. Remember to validate your feelings by asking yourself these questions: "What am I feeling," "Why am I feeling this way?" "What were the circumstances that caused me to feel this way?" "How often do I feel this way," and "Who am I emulating?"

14. Work through negative emotions as soon as they emerge.

15. Listen to what the other person is saying to you. When in doubt, ask for clarification.

16. Listen with the intent to understand. Repeat back to the other person in your words what you think you heard.

17. Notice your body, its space, the body of others and their space.

18. Give others freedom of space and they will honor your space. In addition to learning to manage your anger, it is far better to practice self-control.

Have you felt any of the emotions below?

How do they make you feel about yourself? Write about when you had the feelings below toward someone. Then go through the other exercises to be in better control of your bothersome emotions

Anger —

Revenge —

Jealousy —

Resentment —

How do you feel after expressing the emotions above?

a) Do you feel happy, tired or sad? Write about your feelings.

b) If you felt good, why?

c) How do you feel when you hurt others?

d) How do you feel when others hurt you?

For one week, monitor your inner self-talk and outer behavior.

Record your daily results below.

Write the words you use when talking with others about your anger. Write down your bodily reactions: breathing, clenched teeth, heavy breathing, tight neck or shoulder muscles, tight jaws, hot ears or other body parts, rigid, tense body posture, balled fist, rolled eyes. Write any other bodily reactions you have that I did not list.

1. **Day one:**

2. **Day two:**

3. **Day three:**

4. **Day four:**

5. **Day five:**

6. **Day six:**

7. **Day seven:**

Always assume responsibility for what you are feeling, and own all your feelings, including anger. Unresolved anger turns into resentment, envy, jealousy, revenge, and hatred. There is always an underlying feeling of inadequacy when you are angry.

Anger moves through the following stages if it is not resolved immediately:

Frustration→ Unmet Needs/Disappointment→
Embarrassment→ Guilt → Fear of Rejection

1. **Frustration** —unfulfilled expectations. To prevent anger change your goal or plan.

2. **Unmet Needs/Disappointment** — your unfulfilled expectations. To prevent anger, look into the situation, get the facts.

3. **Embarrassment** — expected self-image unfulfilled. Solution: create new self-image.

4. **Guilt** — social expectations you have accepted. Solution, confront the situation behavior or change it.

5. **Fear of rejection** — unknown expectations with probability of consequence. Solution: confront the situation/person/ behavior, explore the cause then decide if you want to avoid the behavior that causes the problem.

Complete the lists below
    1.   List the people to whom you can go when you need help.

2. List the reference books you know how to use (e.g. dictionary, encyclopedia).

3. List the places in your city where you can call on the phone or go for information.

4. List four questions that you don't know where to get information.

COMMUNICATION DEVELOPMENT
Strategies to Deal with Anger/Anger Deflection Techniques

1. Reasoning With Yourself:

Ask yourself, "Is my anger justified?" "Should I do something better," or "Is the situation too unimportant to be worth bothering me?"

The ABCs of Reasoning with Yourself:

A. Conduct a roadmap dialogue with yourself to decide whether the situation merits your continued attention, whether your thought/feeling/urge is justified, and whether you have an effective response.

B. If you answer **No** to any of these questions and prefer not to be upset, try to talk yourself out of the thought, feeling or urge.

C. If you remain angry, consider if your anger is worth the physiological costs to your health. If necessary, quickly move to other strategies.

2. Thought Stopping:

We have all been programmed to react to certain instances in certain ways. By using the technique to thought stopping, we lay the groundwork to begin to change our programming.

The ABCs of Thought Stopping:

A. Decide if your anger does not merit your further attention is unjustified, or you have no effective response.

B. Depending on the circumstances, silently or aloud, yell "STOP."

C. If the thought, feeling, or urge is now gone or less demanding of your attention, congratulate yourself on having successfully lowering your hostility; otherwise move on to another strategy.

3. Distract Yourself:

Our consciousness has difficulty focusing on two subjects at once. When we start thinking about something new, we stop thinking about what is making us angry. By distracting our attention away, we short-circuit the hostility.

The ABCs of Distracting Yourself:

A. After deciding that there is no effective way to change an anger-arousing situation, choose a distraction.

B. Take "time out" from the situation by devoting your attention to some less-annoying focus – a magazine, television program, people-watching, or a fantasy.

C. If you succeed, reward yourself with a mental pat on the back. If distraction doesn't work, proceed to another strategy.

4. Avoid Over-stimulation:

Hostile persons are often in a highly agitated state. This state may be further heightened by nicotine, caffeine, sweets or drugs and alcohol. Using less of these substances can help reduce anger.

The ABCs to Avoid Over-Stimulation:

A. Make it a goal to cut back as much as you can or to eliminate nicotine, caffeine, sweets, alcohol or drugs.

B. Set another goal, e.g. exercising several times a week.

C. Congratulate yourself when you achieve these goals; accept that it is common to fail, and when you do, simply begin anew.

LET GO OF DEFENSIVE COMMUNICATION

A. Let go defensive or caustic words

You don't need them. There are better ways to reinforce yourself, than with hostile words. Nothing really gets defended OR preserved by them

B. Live by this formula: 2 + 2 = 10 times 1.

Your two ears (listening) and your two eyes (attending and focusing) are usually far more (10 times) valuable when leading and trying to influence persuasively than your one mouth, however articulate.

C. Train your tongue to avoid clichés.

I know how you feel, but…   You just don't understand…
Well, I'm not perfect, so…   What's your problem, anyway?

D. Keep your cool under fire.

One year from now will it matter? Try the earthquake safety slogan: "Duck, cover and hold."

You yourself are not (usually) the target. Accept one of the facts of life — that life is not fair. Resolving to and/or doing good does not grant us full coverage. Like health insurance, there are high deductible and co-payments to sustained success in competitive situations.

E. The more complex an interchange, the more important it is to listen.

It's hard to make a mistake or hurt someone's feelings when listening.

CHALLENGING ERRONEOUS BELIEFS THAT MAY CAUSE YOU TO OVER-REACT

Ask yourself the following questions
1. How do I know this will happen?
2. What proof do I have?
3. Is it 100 percent true?
4. Will the horrible consequence happen?
5. How do I know the consequence will happen?
6. Is it catastrophic?
7. Will I collapse, fall apart, die?
8. Will I be abandoned, rejected?
9. How do I know this for sure?
10. What do I know about my ability to handle or change the threatening consequences?
11. Ask yourself am I worthless or bad? If so:
    • All of me? How much of me? Who says so?
    • Where did I learn this?
    • Am I collecting rubber bands?
    • Do I really believe this?
    • What evidence do I have to counter this?
12. Am I powerless, helpless if this happens?

The Emotions Found Under Anger

Our two basic emotions are Pain and Pleasure.
   Pain that occurs in the Present is perceived as Hurt.
   Pain that occurs in the Past is seen as Anger.
   Pain that occurs in the Future is seen as Anxiety.
   Unexpressed Anger that is held within shows up as Guilt.

Anger Management Log

Name ....

Fill out this log each time you find yourself in an anger-provoking situation.

1. What was the situation? Who was involved?

2. On a scale of 1–5, how angry was I?
       a) Irritated —
       b) Ticked off —
       c) Upset —
       d) Extremely angry —
       e) Major blow-up —

3. What did you say or do to respond?

4. Was this response appropriate or inappropriate: Yes/No? Why?

5. What was the consequence of your response?
   Did you get what you wanted?

6. Is this a healthy or unhealthy behavior pattern?

How to Respond to Others' Anger

Listen actively:
- Make eye contact.
- Move to general area.
- Let person vent.
- Paraphrase what person says:

    "Let me make sure I understand you...."

    "You are concerned about...."

Do not take situation personally.

Acknowledge the feelings of others.

"I can see that you feel strongly about this. We can discuss this further at the break."

Maintain eye contact.

"You are shouting. This is inappropriate behavior. Let's discuss this at.....o'clock tomorrow,"

(or after work; at our break; at home after dinner; after the kids go to bed.)

What is an Anger Workout

A key point to remember is that your anger work-out process is on-going. We have to work out our frustration and anger, just as we work out our body muscles. When you stop doing any of the work-outs, your old counterproductive anger habits are likely to reemerge. The more you work-out, the less chance there is to be hurt by your old anger habits. Eventually, you will be able to do the work-outs on an automatic basis. When this happens you will be more productive in all aspects of your life. You will be a more loving person, a better student, friend, associate, and parent, a more effective worker, and live longer. Working out your anger shapes you for life.

Learning to control your anger helps you to:
1. Recognize your temperament.
2. Validate your temperament.
3. Learn to delay action on your temper.
4. Label and verbalize your feelings.
5. Think about your options.
6. Empathize with others.

HOW TO USE AN ANGER MANAGEMENT WORKOUT?
Three essential emotional components of anger are:
1. **Thoughts**
2. **Bodily responses**
3. **Behavior.**

Your skill in managing these components will help you control your anger, which is a prerequisite for working it out. Anger Workout is a technical work-out, so take your time doing it.

This anger workout
Is recommended for:
1. People who want to control their anger
2. People who have trouble with their emotions
3. People who want to learn about their emotions
4. People who want to take charge of their emotions.

ANGER WORKOUT NOTES
An important assumption of the workout process is that the full experience of your anger (an emotional state) must include a fusion of your *thoughts, actions,* and *reactions.* When these components are disassociated, we are left with something other than a true "anger state", e.g. frustration or hurt.

WHAT MAKES ME MAD
Answer the questions below.

Five people I get mad at are:

............................, ..., ...

.... and ....

I get mad at them because:

....

....

I think people get mad at me in the same way.

They get mad at me because ....

....

....

I can stop making people mad by

....

....

....

Start your anger workout now.

Select an emotional component which causes you trouble today:

1. Thoughts (words)

2. Bodily responses

3. Behavior

I want to/am willing to change the above:

Therefore I will do the following:

Describe a time when you felt each of the emotions listed below:

1. I felt FRUSTRATED when

....

....

2. I felt LONELY when

....

....

3. I felt EXCITED when

....

....

4. I felt NERVOUS when

....

....

5. I felt ANGRY when

....

....

6. I felt SCARED when

....

....

7. I felt SORRY when

....

....

8. I felt DISAPPOINTED when

....

....

HOW TO MANAGE YOUR ANGER

1. Anger does not have to be released like steam in a pressure cooker. Learn to release your anger slowly, over time.

2. Venting/expressing your anger makes you feel better only for a moment, then regret, disappointment and sorrow follow an emotional outburst.

3. The first step is to figure out what is causing you to get angry or react in an angry way.
   a. What are you saying to yourself?
   b. Do you feel victimized, taken advantage of, disrespected, ignored or not acknowledged?

c. Do you have a fear of rejection?

d. Do you like yourself? People who like themselves do not need to prove to someone else that they are right.

e. People who like themselves do not take or interpret things others say to them as a personal offense. You can give the other person the benefit of the doubt or let things pass without responding.

PATIENCE

The qualities of patience and understanding are much needed in our world. I contribute to the fulfilling of this need by being patient with myself and others, and I give understanding to all.

My capacity for patience increases as I express an attitude of understanding.

I find new understanding and greater insight in my daily giving and living by having a patient attitude.

Patience and understanding contribute to the sharing of my thoughts and ideas with others. And the relationships in my life are blessed because of this. Being patient and understanding, gives me a greater sense of oneness with God.

ON REBELLION

Rebellion against your faults,
shortcomings and handicaps,
gets you nowhere.
Self-pity gets you nowhere.
One must have the adventure and
Daring to accept oneself
As a bundle of possibilities
And undertake the most
Interesting game in the world
Making the most of one's best

HARRY EMERSON FREDRICK

AWARENESS WHEEL

1. When you do…
   When you say…

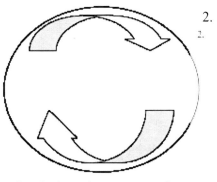

4. Restate
   "In the future…
   (Specify what
   you need or
   want)

2. I feel…
   Hurt…
   Angry…
   Abused…
   Used…
   Frustrated…
   Afraid…
   Disgusted…
   Etc.

3. Is that what you mean?
   (Yes) Resolve or drop it
   (No) Clarify

Your Personality Style Inventory
Test Your Personal Style
What percentage of time do you do the following?
Mark each one 25%, 50%,75%, 100% of the time.
Introvert

Are you moody.. __

Like to be alone .... __

Difficult to talk to people .... __

Difficult to express myself................................... __

Think about myself .... __

Uncomfortable with new people .... __

Preoccupied with myself...................................... __

Serious natured.. __

Have outside interest other than my routine work ..... __

Quiet when angry .... __

Concerned about what people think about me .... __

Total... __

Extrovert

Happy Personality .... __

Smile easily .... __

Easy to talk to new people .... __

Comfortable with people...................................... __

Good outlook on life .... __

Loud when angry... __

Anger easily .... __

Concerned what others think about me.................. __

Do you do extra things for others......................... __

Enjoy doing for others .... __

Think about others... __

Total... __

Tally your total percentage................................. __

Advice from a Parent to Her Child

"Good Enough"

I can teach you things, but I cannot make you learn.
I can give you directions, but I cannot always be there to lead you.
I can allow you freedom, but I cannot account for it.
I can take you to Church, but I cannot make you believe.
I can teach you right from wrong, but I cannot always decide for you.
I can buy you beautiful clothes, but I cannot make you lovely inside.
I can offer you advice, but I cannot accept it for you.
I can teach you about friends, but I cannot choose them for you.
I can advise you about sex, but I cannot keep you pure.
I can tell you the facts of life, but I cannot build your reputation.
I can tell you about drink, but I cannot say no for you.
I can warn you about drugs, but I cannot prevent you from using them.
I can tell you about lofty goals, but I cannot achieve them for you.
I can teach you about kindness, but I cannot force you to be gracious.
I gave you life, but I cannot live it for you.

REFLECTIONS ON ANGER

Our internal feelings are ongoing. There is something inside us that is the same no matter what happens to us on the outside. When someone insults you, focus yourself so that you are just listening to them, not doing anything, not reacting to what they say, you are just listening. If someone insults you or someone praises you, learn to just listen to them. Do not be concerned whether it is an insult, praise, honor or dishonor; just listen. You will get disturbed on the outside, so look at that. Do not try to change it. Notice how you feel when you are angry, remain focused in your center to look at the core being of yourself. Develop a detachment that is not forced, but is spontaneous and natural. Once you have the feeling of a natural detachment, nothing will be able to disturb you.

In a village where the great Zen master Hakuin was living, a girl became pregnant. Her father bullied her for the name of her lover; in the end, to escape punishment she told him it was Hakuin. The father said no more, but when the time came and the child was born, he at once took the baby to Hakuin and threw it down. "It seems that this is your child," he said, and he piled on every insult and sneer at the disgrace of the affair.

Hakuin only said, "Oh, is that so?" and took the baby in his arms. Wherever he went thereafter, he took the baby, wrapped in the sleeve of his ragged robe. During rainy days and stormy nights he would go out to beg milk from the neighboring houses. Many of his disciples turned against him and left. Hakuin did not say a word.

Meantime, the mother found she could not bear the agony of separation from her child. She confessed the name of the real father, and her own father rushed to Hakuin and prostrated himself, begging over and over for forgiveness. Hakuin said only, "Oh, is that so?" and gave him the child back.

The man without his own opinions cares what others say, because he has no thoughts of his own. Whatever he thinks he is, is just a collection of opinions of other people. Somebody has said, "You are beautiful," someone has said, "You are intelligent," and he collects all these. Therefore he is always afraid he should not behave in a way that he loses his reputation, or respectability. He is always afraid of public opinion, what people will say, because all he knows about himself is what people have said about him. If they take their opinions back, they leave him naked. Then he will not know who he is; he asks him/herself, am I ugly, beautiful, intelligent, or unintelligent? He has no idea of his own being because he has learned to depend on others for his definition of who he is and how he should think about himself.

The person of greatness has no need of others' opinions. He knows himself, so it does not matter what others say. Even if the whole world says something that goes against his own experience, he will simply laugh, because he knows inwardly that it is not true.

A Hopi Elder Speaks

*"You have been telling people that this is the Eleventh Hour. Now you must go back and tell the people that this **is** the hour and there are things to be considered:*

"Where are you living?

"What are you doing?

"What are your relationships?

"Are you in right relationships with others?

"Where is your water?

"Do you know your garden? It is time to speak your truth?

"Create your community. Be good to each other. And do not look outside yourself for the leader"

Then he clasped his hands together, smiled, and said, "This could be a good time. There is a river flowing now very fast. It is so great and swift that there are those who will be afraid. They will try to hold on to the shore. They will feel they are being torn apart and will suffer greatly. Know the river has its destination. The elders say we must let go of the shore, push off into the middle, of the river. Keep your eyes open and your heads above the water. I say, see who is in there with you and celebrate. This time in history we are to take nothing personally, least of all, ourselves. For the moment we do, our spiritual growth and our journey come to a halt. It is the time that the lone wolf is over. It is time to gather yourselves and banish the world struggle from your attitude and your vocabulary. Let all that we do now must be done in a sacred manner and in celebration."

THE BENEFITS OF MANAGING YOUR ANGER

A key point to remember is that your anger work-out process is on-going. We have to work o1ut our frustration and anger just we work out our body muscles. When you stop doing any of the work-outs, your old counterproductive anger habits are likely to reemerge. The more you work out, the less chance there is to be hurt by your old anger habits. Eventually, you will be able to do the work-outs on an automatic basis. My prayer is that you live a long, stress free, fruitful life, and achieve all your goals and aspirations. Anger is neither good nor bad. It is just an emotion. When used wisely, it can allow you to be a powerful person, who is a pleasure to be around.

Steps to learn self-control

1. Notice when you are too hyperactive and unable to focus your thought (attention) or energy (nervous, fidgety).

2. When you are too hyperactive to think, or be calm, take deep breaths, breathe deeply for three minutes or count to ten, three times.

3. Learn to organize your immediate environment by keeping things in order. Put things back as you find them, to help create order and stability for yourself.

How you can become unstoppable by anger

1. Never allow fear to prevent you from trying.

2. Realize that only you control what you can become.

3. Tolerate pain and you will hurt less.

4. Try new ways.

5. Accept that
   a) Your only accomplishments are what you have overcome
   b) Gifts are the opposite of achievements

6. Believe tomorrow will be better

ACTIONS AND THOUGHTS TO HELP YOU REENERGIZE YOUR LIFE
:

1. Work on being congruent on both inside and outside yourself.

2. Learn to organize your immediate environment.

3. Put things back as you find them to help create order and stability for yourself.

4. Seek to be the same all the time.

5. Learn to organize your life by keeping a daily "To Do List." Divide all your daily activities into A, B, C, D, according to their importance. Give 'A' activities highest priority, etc.

6. Never settle for less than the best effort, best preparation, best outcome, then give it your best follow through.

7. Be your own coach.

8. Push yourself to be your best, and tell yourself you can.

9. Others may provoke you to anger, but you do not have to respond angrily.

10. When you do what others want, they have the power to control you.

11. No one is the cause of you responding angrily. You have freedom of choice.

12. When you get mad, you are exercising your power or seek to avenge yourself.

13. If you get angry repeatedly, you get some pleasure from hurting others.

14. If you get angry repeatedly, you are unable to control your feelings of anger.

15. To keep your anger under control, do a kind act each day for yourself and someone else.

16. Give yourself permission to be gentle with yourself and others; easy does it.

17. Practice ways to be gentle, and kind to yourself and others.

18. Do deep breathing exercises ten minutes, two times a day.

19. Learn to meditate, and practice it for twenty minutes, twice a day
.

These techniques are listed in the book my book, *Light the Fire Within You.*

My Self

I have to live with myself, and so
I want to be fit for myself to know
I want to be able, as days go by,
Always to look myself straight in the eyes;
I don't want to stand, with the setting sun,
And hate myself for the things I've done,
I don't want to keep on a closet shelf,
A lot of secrets about myself.
And fool myself, as I come and go,
into thinking that nobody else will know
The kind of person that I really am;
I don't want to dress up myself in shame.
I want to go out with my head erect,
I want to deserve all men's respect;
But here in the struggle for fame and self,
I want to be able to like myself.
I don't want to look at myself and know
That I'm bluster and bluff and empty show,
I never can hide myself from me;
I see what others may never see;
I know what others may never know;
I never can fool myself, and so, whatever happens,
I want to be Self-respecting and conscience free.

EDGAR A. GUEST

Chapter 4

Domestic Violence

DOMESTIC VIOLENCE PROGRAM
1. Anger Management and Aggressive Behavior Control
2. Communication Skills
3. Conflict Resolution
4. Control Plan
5. Cultural and Societal Basis for Violence
6. Cycle of Violent or Abuse Behavior
7. Impact of Domestic Violence on Children
8. Impact of Substance Abuse
9. Intergenerational Learned Patterns of Violence
10. Intimacy in Relationships
11. Male Role Socialization and Its relationships to Violence
12. Myths about Domestic Violence
13. Non-Violence and Equality in relationships
14. Personal and Cultural Attitudes Toward the Opposite Sex
15. Personal Responsibility for Violence
16. Stress Management
17. Tactics of Power and Control
18. The Relationships of Guilt and Shame to Violence
19. Time-outs

DOMESTIC VIOLENCE DEFINED
What Is Abuse?
Domestic violence is defined as the abuse of family members or family violence, or any act, whether of omission or commission, that is physically, emotionally, sexually, and/or psychologically harmful and is intended to achieve power and control over the victim. Family violence often involves a

70

pattern of controlling behavior reinforced by violence or its threat.

CHILD ABUSE

Can be sexual, neglectful (failure to provide nourishment), physical (beating, hitting, whipping with a belt, stick or object that breaks the skin or causes bleeding/bruising).

Physical Abuse — Hitting with the hand/fist or object that breaks the skin or cause bleeding or bruising.

Sexual Abuse — Is an unwanted/uninvited sexual intercourse; penetration into the vagina of a child under the age of 18.

Emotional/Psychological Abuse — Tormenting or continued emotional distress inflicted upon a person, against their will.

Neglect — Often refers to a parent/caretaker who fails to provide for the welfare of a minor child in their custody, allowing them to go without food clothing or shelter.

Child Witnessing Domestic Violence — A child is traumatized by being exposed to fights or arguments between the adults caring for him/her. The child will act out later in life what they experience as a child.

SPOUSAL ABUSE

Physical abuse — May include slapping, pushing, choking, and punching.

Emotional/ Psychological — Includes name calling and put-downs. Threats or intimidation are used to instill fear.

Isolation — The person is controlling who he/she associates with and/or where he/she goes.

Economic abuse — Is keeping a spouse in the dark about finances or making financial decisions without spouse's consent.

"Male" or Executive Privilege — Includes a husband treating his wife as a servant or acting like the "master" of the house.

Programs Available to Assist with Family Violence
• Support Group for Victims
• Group Therapy for perpetrators or victims
• Individual Counseling
• Stress & Anger Management
• New Parent Support Program
• Use of Community Resources

Communication Patterns to Prevent Domestic Violence

Leveling and Editing
Leveling and editing are two basic skills you can use to improve your relationships

Leveling
Leveling means letting your partner know what you are feeling by announcing your thoughts clearly and simply. It means that you can be transparent in communicating where you stand and candid in signaling where you want to go.
When you speak in "I-messages" and follow the other principles of good communication, you are leveling.

Editing
Strange as it may seem, one of the first things to go in intimate relationships is the very courtesy and politeness that we are quite likely to continue to pay to total strangers. You wouldn't think of interrupting a stranger to say "Good heavens. Are you going to tell that old story again?" Nor would you indiscriminately snap at someone at work if you were depressed. There is a kind of disregard that is easily adopted toward the feelings of a partner. Each partner is likely to say, "If the you would be more considerate of my feelings, then I would be more considerate of your feelings, but not until then." No

one is willing to start being considerate all alone, but it is important to start somewhere. That is where editing comes in.

Editing means choosing to be polite. Like an actual newspaper editor, you choose to leave certain things out. This means consciously omitting certain hurtful statements, often at the same time that your partner is being most unrealistic and impolite. Editing can be hard, but it is also a very valuable skill.

When to level and when to edit

Editing may be particularly useful for you right now if you are constantly arguing with or insulting your partner or wanting to have the last word. On the other hand if you feel distant from someone that you would like to feel closer to, *leveling* may be what you need to do. When you combine the two skills and achieve a balance between them, communication is more effective than when you use just one skill exclusively.

Adapted from: *A Couples Guide to Communication* by Dr. John Gottman, Howard Markman, Jonni Gonso, Clifford Notarius (Champaign: Research Press, 1976).

CONFLICT CONTAINMENT

Three Types of Relationship Conflict:

- **First** – Addresses a specific **issue** or complaint, for example "You came home late without calling and I'm mad."

- **Second** – Attacks the *person* rather than the problem or issue. Using words like "never," "always" and "if you really love me" show up as guilt. For example, "if you really loved me, you would stay home tonight."

- * **Third** – Attacks the **relationship**. Once you have a second degree conflict and have put the other person down, it's only a stone throw away form the attacking the relationship. Why continue staying with someone who is worth so little? Divorce threats are made during times of anger, not because the person really wants to leave, but because the conflict has escalated. Once the threat has been made, it is too easy for partners to start talking about a divorce or separation that neither really wants.

To contain relationship conflicts, it is important for both partners to keep their conflicts at the first level and to avoid escalating to the second or third level. If you find yourself escalating the conflict, attacking your partner, or threatening to leave when you really don't intend to do so, try to "catch yourself in the act," or as soon afterwards as you can. You can then de-escalate the conflict at the level of the original issue.

Adapted from: *Helping Couples Change* by Richard Stuart, (New York: Guilford Press, 1980)

THE SIX STAGES OF RELATIONSHIP CONFLICT
1. Triggers

Triggers are cues that "set you off." They are the external incidents or situations, the behaviors on your partner's part, and your internal feeling or thoughts that precede getting angry. For example, your dinner date is late or your mother-in-law is visiting might be external trigger situations. A tightened jaw or quickened pulses are examples of internal triggers. At the trigger stage, your reaction is under voluntary control, even though there is increased likelihood of conflict in the near future. The advantage of recognizing triggers early in the sequence of events is that this recognition can help you *prevent* the conflict in that same way that a "Fire danger is high in the forest" sign warns you to be particularly careful with matches. Some effective strategies for interrupting the conflict pattern are to simply refuse to be drawn into an argument or to isolate yourself from your partner temporarily at the trigger stage.

2. Lashing Out

In the lashing out stage, sudden burst of anger erupt. Name calling, swear words, physical violence, and hurtful accusations and threats can be hurled almost reflexively, without rational thought. Later, the person often regrets his or her actions. It is crucial to stop and get away from any physical violence at this point. This is not the time for problem solving, and if you attempt problem solving or rational discussion at this moment, you may even increase the other person's anger.

3. A Lull in the Action

Strong reflexive actions cannot be maintained for very long. The initial surge of anger is followed by a dip in the intensity of the emotion. This is an opportunity to interrupt the conflict cycle.

4. An Uneasy Quiet

At the next stage there is a certain feeling of unrest. Anger is kept alive not so much by the original insult as by self-talk, thoughts such as, "I shouldn't stand for that." One struggles between two feelings, the desire to get back at the other person, and the wish to let the issue die quietly. During this stage, behavior is often cunning, planned, and manipulative; frequently there is withdrawal. The way one handles this stage of the argument can greatly shorten the period of battle or increase the level of negativity in the relationship. During this stage, the issue at hand is much less important than the management of the conflict. One or both partners feel wronged, and the best thing that can happen at this stage is to keep it as short as possible. Changing the scene can help to break the grip of the anger; for example, if the radio is on, someone might turn it off; if it is off, it can be turned on. This stage can last minutes, days, or weeks, until one person reaches out to the other.

5. Reaching Out

At this stage, couples shift from the argument phase to the problem-solving phase. At first, movements toward this stage may be so tentative that they may be overlooked or misperceived. When this happens, the partner who is reaching out may feel frustrated and return to an earlier stage or begin a new attack. To prevent this from happening, couples can develop a signal system to indicate their readiness to lay anger aside and go on. For example, one person might enter the room and take the partner's hand; the partner signals reaching out by squeezing the hand and not pulling away.

3. Laying the Anger Aside

This is the point at which the argument ends and both partners lay their anger aside. Problem-solving does not always need to take place right away, but it should take place soon in order to prevent the situation from happening again. If problem solving does not take place, conflict will probably recur when the trigger is present in the future and the cycle will begin again.

Adapted from: *Helping Couples Change* by Richard Stuart, (New York: Guilford Press, 1980)

THE CYCLE OF DOMESTIC VIOLENCE

If you understand the cyclical nature of domestic abuse and violence, it may help you deal with it in your own life. Abuse and violence in a domestic setting often comes in cycles. These cycles were identified and described in 1979 by Dr. Lenore E. Walker in her book *The Battered Woman.*

Phase One: The Build-Up This is the "walking on eggs" part, where you know trouble is brewing and building. There is tension in the air. The tension escalates. Some women actually provoke a blow-up to end the tension.

Phase Two: The Blow-Up This is the peak of violence. It may be a verbal tirade, throwing things, or a physical attack, depending on where you are on the continuum of escalating violence.

Phase Three: Remorse and Contrition He feels sorry for what he has done. He apologizes; he promises that he will never do it again. He promises to change. He may bring gifts. He can be very charming, charismatic, and persuasive. He might bring you gifts and flowers. He may promise to go to counseling with you, and he may go. This is the honeymoon, the seduction. You are hopeful that he will truly change.

Dr. Walker notes that the one thing all women reported of their batterers was their manipulative charm in this phase.

You fear him, you love him, and you are hopeful. You take him back. Then he begins to get restless, and the tension starts building again. These phases repeat and keep repeating until the cycle is broken.

LIST OF ESCALATING BEHAVIORS

This is about behavior that is repeated. A truly rare bad episode is not at all the same thing as a recurring pattern.

1. Disrespect, attacks on your self-esteem.

- He is disrespectful in the way he speaks to you. For example, he calls you derogatory names. He criticizes the way you look and what you do in a destructive way. He acts as if you can't do anything right and you begin to believe him. You lose your self-confidence and sense of self-worth.
- When something goes wrong, he blames you. Everything is your fault. He is frequently suspicious and accuses you of wrongdoing.
- He yells at you and swears at you.
- He makes humiliating, embarrassing, or belittling remarks. He makes them in from of others. He ridicules you, your friends and your family.
- He erupts into tirades, violent fits of screaming anger.
- He takes his own bad behavior very lightly. What are you so upset about? He didn't abuse you, you provoked him. It's all your fault. He shifts responsibility away from himself and blames you.

2. Pressure, manipulation and control

After disrespect comes control. This is the next step toward more apparent forms of violence. He is pushing you around mentally and verbally.

- He interrupts, refuses to listen or to take seriously what you have to say.
- He twists what you say, and turns your words against you.
- He tells you what to do, and tries to make you feel bad, guilty or wrong if you do not do what he wants.
- He insists that his ideas are "right," and that you are wrong.
- What he says is the "truth" he says that you are confused.
- He rushes you into making decisions.
- He pouts and sulks if you do not do what he wants.
- He uses the children against you. He teaches them to be disrespectful of you. They are conflicted and do not understand why.
- He shapes your life. He knows what is best for you; he acts as your teacher and guide. You believe he knows what is best and your judgment becomes replaced by his.

3. Economic control, Isolation

Economic control and isolation can become imprisonment.

- He refuses to let you work. He undermines or interferes with your work, either subtly or overtly. He refuses to let you go to school or start a career.
- He is the sole support of the family and refuses to give you money. If you have any money, he takes it or controls the amount you can have.
- He takes your car or your car keys, or otherwise prevents you from getting around.
- He controls your time, and who you spend time with. He tells you who you can see, where you can and can't go.
- He monitors phone calls and insists on knowing where you have been. You have to account for you time.
- He frequently checks up on you.

Some abusive partners control diplomatically, but nevertheless they control you. They arrange circumstances and finances so that you can't make a move without their approval. They do not yell or scream, but you are still controlled and imprisoned. If you feel trapped, it is probably because you are trapped. If this is your situation, be alert to the other behaviors listed here and the risk of escalation discussed below.

4. Harassment, repetition, hounding

Some people are obsessive or inappropriate in other ways. This can manifest itself as repetition: he repeats his statements over and over until he wears you down.

- He makes uninvited visits or calls.
- He refuses to leave when asked
- He follows you.
- He embarrasses you in public.

5. Signals of increasing danger

The following behaviors are clear indications that the situation is escalating and the danger increasing. The behavior is becoming more physical, and if he throws something at you one day, he could throw *you* the next.

- Physical menacing or intimidation
- He makes angry or threatening gestures.
- He towers over you in a menacing way
- He stands in a doorway during an argument, or corners you, blocking your escape.
- He drives recklessly while you are in the car.
- He throws things, breaks things, punches the wall, kicks in a door, and throws something out the window.

6. Threats

- He threatens you or your family. If he does this, you must take these threats seriously.

8. Pushing and shoving

Pushing or shoving is the beginning of more direct physical violence. If this is tolerated, the violence will escalate. This is the phase where he is testing limits to see what he can get away with. Many men do not regard this as physical, violent abuse, but *you* know it is.

9. Sexual pressure, assaults

Has he forced you to have sex when you did not want to? Has he forced you to perform sexually in ways degrading to you or against your will? If you tolerate this kind of behavior, it can escalate into direct physical attack and serious physical injury.

10. Physical violence

When you are being hit, kicked, choked, or handled in a violent way, you are being abused. If you continue to tolerate such violence and abuse, it can escalate and become lethal.

11. Weapons
- He has weapons around the house that frighten you.
- He threatens to use them against you.

12. Self-Destructive Behavior

Does he abuse drugs or alcohol? Substance abuse is dangerous because an intoxicated person has little self-control, and there is a greater potential for violence.

Has he threatened suicide? Has he sabotaged his work by not showing up, performing badly, or telling off his boss? It is also self-destructive behavior. Self-destructive behavior and self-sabotage indicate depression and hopelessness; his behavior may be the result of acute mental distress.

Drugs, alcohol, weapons, hopelessness, acute mental distress; all these are indicators that the violence could become lethal.

13. Signals of extreme danger

The following are indicators that an abuser is extremely dangerous and may become seriously violent or kill.

- He has threatened to kill himself, you, the children, or family members.
- He is acutely depressed.
- He has weapons and has used them or threatened to use them.
- He is obsessive about you. He idolizes you, and feel that he cannot live without you. He believes that he is entitled to you.
- Extreme jealousy. He believes that there is another man, and if he cannot have you, no one else can.
- Hopelessness. He feels if he loses you he has lost all hope for a future.
- Extreme rage. The most life-endangering rage is said to arise when the woman leaves and that the first two months are the most dangerous. No one really knows exactly when this "critical" phase starts or ends. We *do* know that leaving this type of person must be planned and carried out with great care.

DEVELOPING LISTENING SKILLS

Critical factors required are:

1. Healthy functioning cerebral cortex, free from chemicals and drugs. You need to have your mind focused on what the other person is saying to you and have a desire to hear what is being said by the other person.

2. We need to see the person who is speaking to us; to have a vision of 20/20 is best, however, if you need to wear corrective eye glasses to see people, then take the necessary measure to get them. Watch the person's lips as they speak to you. This gives you, and them, the added assurance that you have heard what was said.

3. Hearing — We hear best when there is no infection, ear wax build up or obstacle that would prevent us from hearing what is said to us.

4. Healthy functioning body — We do not hear well if our body is in pain, if we are tired, sleepy hung over from drinking alcohol or staying up late without adequate rest; nor do we listen well if we are hungry or need to go to the bathroom.

5. Healthy Emotions — We need to be in control of the following emotions: Fear, anxiety, confusion and frustration. The ability to tolerate conflict or ambiguity is necessary so we can process any unpleasant information we may hear.

6. Desire (You want to listen) — We have to know, before the person speaks to us, that there are benefits and hindrances, and how we will process or handle unpleasant information. Keep in mind the Benefit and Hindrances of what the person is saying while he/she is speaking.

7. Self-Esteem — Having high self-esteem gives you the self-concept (belief) and self-worth that you will not be taken advantage of or that your needs will not be addressed. When you have high self-worth, you can listen or give to another without being depleted. You know your boundaries and when they have been violated.

8. Self-confidence gives you self-assurance and helps you suspend doubts and fear of being rejected.

9. Listen to the Inner Self — We each have an inner intuitive voice that continually speaks to us if we allow ourselves to get in touch with the spiritual part of us.

ABUSE SUPPORT GROUP — TOPICS FOR DISCUSSION

Self-Appreciation
1. What can I do to like me?

2. How can I support myself?

3. What can I do to bring out the best in me?

Respond to these statements
1. If you do what you've always done...You'll get what you've always gotten.

2. You don't have to be good to start...But you have to start to be good.

3. You can tell where your commitment is by the results you see!

G^{O D} ,

Grant me the serenity to accept the things
I cannot change
Courage
To change the things I can and
The wisdom to know the difference.
                                    AMEN

Reinhold Niebuhr

THINGS THAT MAKE YOU GO HMMMMM!
Alcohol always lied to me

I drank for courage…and woke up night after night horrified.

I drank for sophistication…and became crude.

I drank to find peace…and ignited a war within myself.

I drank to be friendly…and became argumentative and nasty.

I drank to be sexy…and turned people off.

I drank so that I could relate to others…and I babbled.

I drank to put down loneliness…and found myself retreating more and more into my shell.

I drank to relax…and woke up tense.

I drank to be entertaining…and became an obnoxious clown.

I drank to live more fully…and contemplated suicide.

I drank for adventure…and discovered disaster.

I drank to be more honest…and insulted my friends.

I drank to quiet my nerves…and woke up with hangover jangles.

I drank to feel better…and ended up sick and throwing up.

I drank to have fun…and passed out in the middle of the party.

I drank to pep myself up…and ended up exhausted.

I drank to feel successful…a big shot…but ended up a failure.

I drank for security…and became afraid of my shadow.

I drank to feel better about myself…and ended up hating me.

I drank to prove I could handle alcohol…and ended up knowing it controlled me.

A friend said…

"But surely, now that you've been sober awhile, it would take a lot of alcohol to put you back in that condition.

"Just one drink!" I answered

85

MAN TALK — WOMAN SPEAK

It's true. Men and women speak different languages. So different are our communication styles that it's almost as though women speak French, for instance, and men speak Spanish. We each know a little of the other's language, but not enough for full comprehension.

Here are some of the sex differences that social psychologists have found in language and communication style:

MEN...	WOMEN...
Talk about sports, money, facts, business and events.	Talk about feelings, relationships, people and psychological states.
Use commands to get what they want.	Use requests.
Use and respond to actions more than words in communicating.	Rely on and respond to words in communicating.
Communicate to persuade, argue, control or impress.	Communicate to share, inform, or support, or ingratiate.
Language is factual and action-oriented.	Language is emotional and evaluative.
Emphasize talking rather than listening in conversations.	Emphasize listening and sharing in conversation.
Use pauses in conversations for emphasis.	Use "intensifiers" like *really, terrifically, tremendously*, (for emphasis).
Speak mostly in a monotone.	Use a variety of tones of voice to convey emotion and meaning.
Express feelings directly.	Verbalize feeling indirectly.
Interrupt more in conversation.	Are interrupted more
Tends to get more attention	Speak in tentative terms.
Self-Assured in their speaking	
Speak authoritatively regardless of subject.	

"Keep reaching in…
Towards the more enlightening perspective."
JAFREE

Love/Fear

Coming from LOVE	Coming from FEAR
Responsibility	Victim
Pro-Active	Re-Active
Towards	Away from
Own shadows	Defensive, denial
Growth/Experience Life	Resist change/stay in your comfort zone
Open/Vulnerable	Protected/Attacking
Ask for help	Do it myself
Joy/Bliss/Curiosity/Peaceful	Anger/Sadness/Shame
Abundance/Cooperation/Win-Win	Scarcity/Competition/Win-Lose
Live in the moment	Fear future/Hold onto past
Empower/Mentor	Control/Dominate
Be of service, hear	Use fix
Pain as sensation, information	Pain as suffering, bad
Learn Lessons	Withdraw/Punish
Connection	Isolation
Observations/Evaluation/Choice	Judgment/Control/obligation
Does it work or not?	Is it good or bad?
Is it empowering?	Is it right or wrong?
I could	I should
Vision/Mission	Survival
Seek to understand/Compassion	Judge/Blame
Go through fear	Fight/Flight
[conscious choice]	[unconscious choice]
Grateful	Jealous/Envious/Needy
Intention/Surrender	Expectation/Attachment
Ask for what I want	Manipulate

THE THREE RULES OF HUMAN BEHAVIOR
Based on comments made by James Woods, MD

 **The Golden Rule**: "Do unto others as you would have them do unto you!" (*Mark 6:31 – NIV*) When using the Golden Rule, you are in total control! You are solely responsible for your actions. You treat others as you would like to be treated without expectations of reciprocity. By doing, you feel more self-confident and self-assured. As a result, you have a peace of mind. You know that you are okay because God gives YOU (the YOU that God wants me to be) Acceptance, Approval, Appreciation and Attention — the A-quad.

My Rule "Others should treat me the way that I treat them!" When using the "MY RULE", you give with reciprocity in mind. You expect others to give you the A-quad. When they fail to comply, you feel cheated, frustrated and powerless. You may say, "I didn't treat them that way — how come they treated me that way?" "How dare they!" The madness begins.

 **The Entitlement Rule** "I expected great treatment, regardless of how I treat you!" When using the "Entitlement Rule", you have an enhanced sense of entitlement. You may feel entitled because of your heritage, your past, your status, your education, you money, your job or whatever. Thinking that you are better than others and expect to be treated better is mad!

Some people give or do with the intention of receiving acceptance and approval. Ironically, they are perceived as gullible and taken advantage of. As a result, they feel used, misused and abused. "My Rule" plus reciprocity is unequal to acceptance and approval. When you use "My Rule", you expect others to treat you like you've treated them. When they fail to reciprocate your good deed, then you get mad!

> *"I did it for him —*
> *how come he can't do it for me?"*

Others that use "The Entitlement Rule" expect people to treat them better than they treat themselves. They have an enhanced sense of self. "Regardless, of who you are, you are beneath me." They believe that they deserve better treatment. The madness perpetuates from these assumptions. The "My Rule" and "The Entitlement Rule" are totally based on the actions of others. Since they are unable to control the actions of others, they feel powerless and victimized!

> *"I don't care how I have treated you, you are supposed to*
> *treaty me like a queen (king) – your feelings don't count!"*

To hide those feelings, they mask them with ANGER! I made the word A-N-G-E-R into an anagram to describe how anger masks feelings that you may feel too vulnerable to reveal. Let us look at it:

DOMESTIC VIOLENCE

Domestic violence in the home is associated with increased isolation from the outside world and limited personal freedom and accessibility to resources. Whenever a woman in the home is placed in physical danger or controlled by the threat or use, she is experiencing domestic violence

Forms of Abuse

Domestic violence is an ongoing debilitating experience of physical, psychological and/or sexual abuse of physical force. The risk for abuse is greatest when a woman is separated from supportive networks.

Physical abuse is usually recurrent and escalates in both frequency and severity. It may include the following:
- Pushing shoving, slapping, punching, kicking, choking.
- Assault with a weapon
- Holding, tying down, or restraining her
- Leaving her in a dangerous place
- Refusing to help when she is sick or injured.

Emotional or psychological abuse may precede or psychological abuse may precede or accompany physical violence as a means of controlling through fear and degradation. It may include the following:
- Threats of harm
- Physical and social isolation
- Extreme jealousy and possessiveness
- Deprivation
- Intimidation
- Degradation and humiliation
- Calling her names and belittling her
- False accusations, blaming her for everything.
- Ignoring, dismissing, or ridiculing her needs.
- Lying, breaking promises destroying trust.
- Driving fast and recklessly to frighten and intimidate her.

Sexual abuse in violent relationships is often the most difficult aspect of abuse for women to discuss. It may include any form of forced sex or sexual degradation such as:

- Trying to make her perform sexual acts against her will
- Pursuing sexual activity when she is not fully conscious or is not asked or is afraid to say no.
- Hurting her physically during sex or assaulting her genitals, including use of objects or weapons intravaginally, orally, or anally.
- Forcing her to have sex without protection against pregnancy or sexually transmissible diseases
- Criticizing her and calling her sexually degrading names.

THE CYCLE THEORY OF VIOLENCE

Phase 1 Tension Building
•Minor battering incidents
•His possessiveness jealousy psychological/verbal humiliation and abuse escalates.
•Woman accepts responsibility for controlling his anger by attempting to anticipate his every whim, staying out of his way, and denying her own emotions and needs.
•Tension between the two becomes unbearable.
•This phase could last anywhere from two days to several years.

CYCLE OF VIOLENCE

Phase 2
Acute battering incident
•Severe physical, emotional, psychological, sexual abuse.
•Woman will get beaten regardless of her response to his violence and cruelty by blaming it on the woman's actions or words.
•This phase usually last between two and twenty-four hours.

Phase 3
The Honeymoon Phase
•During this phase the woman' victimization becomes complete.
•Batterer apologizes for his behavior in the previous stages.
•He tries to persuade her that he wants to get help but claims he can only get help is she stays with him.
•Batterer behaves in a charming and loving manner.
•The woman is given a glimpse of her original dream of how wonderful love is. She trades her psychological and physical safety for this temporary dream state. Thus, her self image withers as she copes with the awareness that she is selling herself/her life for brief periods of phase 3 behavior.

91

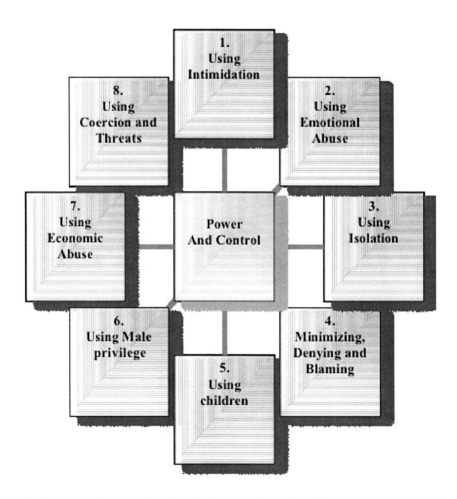

On the next page is a list describing the above squares by number.

1. **Using Intimidation:** Making her afraid by using looks gestures, actions. Smashing things, destroying her property abusing pets displaying weapons.
2. **Using Emotional Abuse:** Putting her down. Making her feel bad about herself. Calling her names. Making her think she's crazy. Playing mind games. Humiliating her. Making her feel guilty.
3. **Using Isolation:** Controlling what she does, who se sees and talks to. What she reads and where she goes. Limiting her outside involvement. Using jealousy to justify actions.
4. **Minimizing denying and blaming:** Making light of the abuse and not taking her concerns about it seriously. Saying the abuse didn't happen. Shifting responsibility for abusive behavior. Saying she caused it.
5. **Using children:** Making her feel guilty about the children. Using the children to relay messages. Using visitation to harass her. Threatening to take the children away.
6. **Using Male Privilege:** Treating her like a servant. Making all the big decisions. Acting like the "master of the castle" Being the one to define mean's and women's roles.
7. **Using Economic Abuse:** Preventing her from getting or keeping a job. Making her ask for money. Giving her an allowance. Taking her money. Not letting her know about or have access to family income.
8. **Using coercion and threats:** Making and or carrying out threats to do something to hurt her. Threatening to leave her, to commit suicide. To report her to welfare. Making her drop charges. Making her do illegal things.

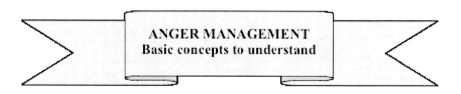

To change your expression of anger, you must change your thinking and re-think change what you say to yourself in your head, in response to the external event.

1. Anger is an emotion.
2. Reason is not employed when we are angry.
3. Anger is the result of jumping to conclusions about an outcome.
4. Anger creates a sense of energy, excitement and negative aliveness.
5. Anger is self-serving.
6. No one is the cause of you responding angrily. You have freedom of choice.
7. Anger is used to intimidate, instill fear, and as an outlet to get rid of one's inner poisons/toxins.
8. You do not have a license to hurt or abuse another with your anger.
9. No one has given you permission to hurt them because of your inability to handle your life's problems.
10. When you are angry, you are out of control not the other person.
11. Others may provoke you to anger, but you do not have to respond angrily. When you respond as others want, they have the power to control you.
12. When you get mad you are exercising your power, or you seek to avenge yourself.
13. You get some pleasure from hurting others, if you get angry repeatedly.
14. If you get angry repeatedly, you are unable to control your feelings of anger.

15. Anger is a powerful emotion, either you control it, or you are controlled by it.
16. Anger is addictive obsessive thinking you can't let go.
17. Anger is about power and control.

ANGER IS A CHOSEN POSITION

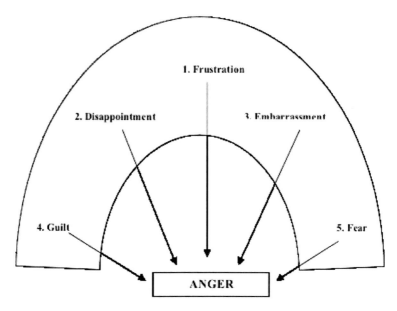

1. **Frustration:** Unfulfilled expectations
   Resolution: Change the goal or change the plan.

2. **Disappointment:** Your unfulfilled expectations
   Resolution: Check it out! Look into it and get the facts.

3. **Embarrassment:** expected self image unfulfilled
   Resolution: Get on with it!

4. **Guilt:** Social/Own expectations you have accepted. Not a guilt
   trip.
   Resolution: Confront. Amend behavior.

5. **Fear:** unknown expectations with probability of consequences.
   Resolution: Confront. Avoid.

Anger can be a signal a caution light to look back at what is causing it. It can turn into resentment which leads to destructive behaviors, and depression. Take responsibility and ownership for your
feelings.

MALE DENIAL SYSTEM OF DOMESTIC VIOLENCE

1. **Simple denial:** "I didn't do it." "I don't remember."

2. **Minimizing:** "I only slapped her, I didn't even close my fist."

3. **Blaming:** "If she wouldn't (whatever), I wouldn't have to hit her."

4. **Rationalizing:** "Her mother was the same way."

5. **Intellectualizing:** "She's just like a child, needs a strong hand and discipline."

6. **Diversion:** Changes the subject to another unrelated topic.

7. **Hostility:** A good defense is a great offense.

INFORMATION AND RESOURCES

If the patient feels it is safe to do so, provide her with written information (including phone numbers) or legal options, local counseling and crisis intervention services, shelter, and community resources. In addition, educational materials on domestic violence in waiting areas and examination rooms may help patients identify violence as a personal health problem.

National organizations on domestic violence and many local and state battered women's programs have information available for use in physician offices. The National Domestic Violence hot line (800 333-SAFE) is a 24 hour resource to help women find local shelters. Counselors speak Spanish as well as English. The National Woman Abuse Prevention Center (202-857-0216) publishes fact sheets on domestic violence, a quarterly newsletter, and a series of brochures. Some of the material is translated into Spanish and Polish. The American College of Obstetricians and Gynecologists (202-863-2518) publishes "The Abused Woman" a publication for patients. The Family Violence Prevention Fund (415-821-4553 provides direct services to victims and develops public policy and training programs. Local domestic violence shelters and statewide domestic violence programs are frequently listed in the phone book. The can help with housing information

KEY CONCEPTS TO HELP YOU MANAGE ANGER

1. Know what makes you angry and what makes others angry.

2. Research your life to see when your feelings were hurt or ignored as a child. Then see if you are getting even with your parents or caretaker.

3. The anger you express as an adult is the unfinished business you have with your parents.

4. We learn to express our anger today from what we saw or experienced as a child.

5. You may be still working thru your adolescent rebellious nature. Check yourself to see if your expression of anger is adult discussion or childish. Argumentation to be right or perfect.

You Can Choose Peace, Harmony and Tranquility

A key point to remember is that your anger work-out process is on-going. We have to work out our frustration and anger just like we work out our body muscles. The more you work out, the less chance there is for anyone to be hurt by your old anger habits. When this happens you will be perceived by others and relate to people differently. You will be a more loving person, a better friend, lover, husband, student, associate, parent, a more effective worker, and live longer. Being in control of your anger gives you choices unavailable to you previously. You can now choose to react angrily or react in a pleasant manner. My prayer is that you live a long, stress free, fruitful life, and achieve all of your goals and aspirations. Anger is neither good nor bad. It is just an emotion. When used wisely, it can allow you to be a powerful person, who is a pleasure to be around.

I coach children, adults, entrepreneurs, and corporations on how to effectively communicate and negotiate to get what you desire. You can reach me at 619-262-9951, www.idagreene.com or email me at: idagreene@idagreene.com We have several books to assist you, they are:

Anger Management Skills For Women,
Anger Management Skills For Men,
How to Improve Self-Esteem In Any Child,
How to Improve Self-Esteem In The African American Child,
Self-Esteem the Essence of You,
Light the Fire Within You,
Soft Power Negotiation Skills,
Money, How to Get It, How To Keep It,
How to Be A Success In Business,
Are You Ready for Success?
Say Goodbye to Your Smallness, Say Hello to Your Greatness, and Stirring Up the African American Spirit.

Bibliography

Gottman, John, Cliff Notarius, Jonni Gonso, and Howard Markman. *A Couple's Guide to Communication.* Champaign: Research Press, 1976

Stuart, Richard. *Helping Couples Change.* New York: Guilford Press, 1980

Tavris, Carol. *Anger: The Misunderstood Emotion.* New York: Touchstone Books, 1989

Walker, Lenore E. *The Battered Woman.* New York: Harper and Row 1979.

CPSIA information can be obtained at www.ICGtesting.com
Printed in the USA
LVOW081551270112

265900LV00004B/162/P